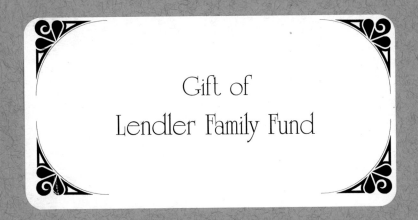

Surviving
Hitler

Also by the Author

Orphan Train Rider: One Boy's True Story
(Boston: Houghton Mifflin, 1996)

Pioneer Girl: Growing Up on the Prairie
(New York: Morrow Junior Books, 1998)

We Rode the Orphan Trains
(Boston: Houghton Mifflin, 2001)

Janek "Jack" Mandelbaum at age eighteen

Surviving Hitler

A BOY IN THE NAZI DEATH CAMPS

by Andrea Warren

HarperCollins*Publishers*

Surviving Hitler
Copyright © 2001 by Andrea Warren
All rights reserved. No part of this book may be used or reproduced in
any manner whatsoever without written permission except in the
case of brief quotations embodied in critical articles and reviews.
Printed in the United States of America. For information address
HarperCollins Childen's Books, a division of HarperCollins Publishers,
1350 Avenue of the Americas, New York, NY 10019.
www.harperchildrens.com

Library of Congress Cataloging-in-Publication Data
Warren, Andrea.
  Surviving Hitler : a boy in the Nazi death camps / by Andrea Warren.
    p.   cm.
  Includes bibliographical references.
  ISBN 0-688-17497-3 — ISBN 0-06-029218-0 (lib. bdg.)
  1. Mandelbaum, Jack—Childhood and youth—Juvenile literature.   2. Jewish children in the Holocaust—
Biography—Juvenile literature.   3. Holocaust, Jewish (1939–1945)—Poland—Gdynia—Personal narratives—Juvenile
literature.   4. Gdynia (Poland)—Biography—Juvenile literature.   [1. Mandelbaum, Jack—Childhood and youth.
2. Jews—Poland—Biography.   3. Holocaust survivors.   4. Holocaust, Jewish (1939–1945)—Poland— Gdynia—
Personal narratives.]   I. Title.
DS135.P63 M289   2001   00-038899
940.53'18'092—dc21   CIP
[B]   AC

Typography by Robbin Gourley
1   2   3   4   5   6   7   8   9   10
❖
First Edition

FOR KYM, MY SHINING LIGHT

Sadly, racial, ethnic, and cultural hatred and intolerance are not just history; they are current events.

—Steven Spielberg
Film director

I have always known my father as a very loving, caring person who is completely devoted to his family. When I visited Poland with him and heard the story of what had happened to him during the war, I understood for the first time what he had lived through. Now that I know what he survived and have seen what he has done with his life, he is my greatest hero.

—Mark Mandelbaum
Jack's son

ACKNOWLEDGMENTS

Like every book, this one has received support, advice, and hands-on help from many people. First and foremost is Jack Mandelbaum, who generously shared not only his memories but also his scholarship and his time. My husband, Jay Wiedenkeller, was, as always, my mainstay while I struggled with difficult subject matter. Barbara Bartocci and Deborah Shouse offered invaluable help. My agent, Regina Ryan, shared my inspiration and commitment to bringing my literary vision to life. Barbara Lalicki, my editor at HarperCollins, and assistant editor Rachel Orr saw me through the rough spots as my manuscript was transformed into this book.

I was also assisted by Chris Sims at the United States Holocaust Memorial Museum; Jean Zeldin, Susan Haws, and Fran Sternberg at the Midwest Center for Holocaust Education; and the archival staff at the Truman Library.

Others to whom I am grateful are Murray (Moniek) Ciesla for his memories, and Pola Firestone, James Levy, Amy Sussna, Lisa Armstrong, David Barash, Debi Fast, Claudia Mandelbaum, and Shirley Sander and the late Sam Sander.

Finally, a very special thank-you to Andrea Curley, my first editor, whose editorial eye and encouragement helped this project take flight.

CONTENTS

These children enjoying themselves in prewar Poland could not have known what was going to happen to their country when it was invaded by Hitler.

Before his sudden death in 1998, Sam Sander of Kansas City opened my eyes to the Holocaust.

In the small Nebraska town where I grew up in the decades following World War II—a war that both my father and uncle fought in—no one talked about the Holocaust, nor did I know anyone who was Jewish. My high school history textbook allotted only a few sentences to this catastrophic event. Photos showing emaciated survivors and the grotesque bodies of the dead suggested such horror that I wanted to stay as far away from the subject as I could.

Then I met Sam. He told me about his terrifying experiences in Hitler's death camps and showed me the tattoo on his arm from Auschwitz. Sam made real the faces in the photos. I looked at them again and saw actual people instead of victims. Each person had once had a good life, people he or she loved, and hopes for a happy future. Then all of them were ensnared in Hitler's frenzied mania to destroy the Jewish race and other "enemies" of the Nazi state.

I began listening to the stories of survivors. When I met Jack Mandelbaum, I knew I wanted to tell his story. Like Sam, Jack spent three years as a teenager in the death camps. He survived through courage, luck, help from others, and sheer will. Like all survivors, he has much to teach us about bravery and self-reliance, and about history and the lessons of the Holocaust.

I have reconstructed this history from fact and from Jack Mandelbaum's experiences. While he has a remarkable memory, he of course could not remember verbatim conversations that took place over sixty years ago. Thus, when you read direct quotes set in the times before and during the war, please be aware that I have exercised literary license, writing them as closely as possible to the way Jack recalled them.

Sometimes from survivors we can gain insight into our own lives. Sam had shown me a letter he received from a student who had listened to him speak at her school. She told him she was having problems at home and school and had tried to kill herself. She had been planning to try again. Then she heard him. Listening to the horrible things he had gone through, she decided that if he could survive what he had, and still create a good life for himself, then she would try to work out her problems. She reported that things were much better now, and she was grateful to him for what she had learned from him.

In spite of how hard it may be for us to hear the survivors' stories, it is even harder for them to tell us. It forces them to relive the nightmare of their brutal and inhumane experiences. But they know we must be warned. People throughout the world continue to do horrible things to one another. We have so much yet to learn. If we will open ourselves to their stories, with the Holocaust survivors as our guides, we can learn to recognize and work to eradicate the roots of racism, discrimination, oppression, and tyranny.

If we do not, who might be the next target of the kind of "ethnic cleansing" practiced by the Nazis? Could it be you?

In Germany they first came for the Communists, and I didn't speak up because I wasn't a Communist. Then they came for the Jews, and I didn't speak up because I wasn't a Jew. Then they came for the trade unionists, and I didn't speak up because I wasn't a trade unionist. Then they came for the Catholics, and I didn't speak up because I was a Protestant. Then they came for me—and by that time no one was left to speak up.

—Reverend Martin Niemöller,
Protestant minister, Germany, and
concentration camp survivor

In the port city of Danzig, now Gdansk, just a few miles from Gdynia, Jack often saw excursion boats ferrying passengers on leisurely outings along the city's canals.

1

ntil he was twelve, Jack Mandelbaum assumed his life would always be a carefree adventure.

He lived with his father, mother, older sister, and younger brother in beautiful Gdynia *(ga-DIN-ya)*, Poland, on the shores of the Baltic Sea.

"Our city was the pride of Poland," Jack recalled, remembering his childhood. "Ships came into port from all over the world. I heard many foreign languages. I saw sailors who wore turbans, and black sailors from Africa. This was just part of my daily life."

Jack collected stamps and begged ship captains for ones from faraway places. He kept his stamps neatly categorized in books and loved to imagine the strange and exotic countries they came from.

His father, Majloch Mandelbaum—"Max" to his friends—was the prosperous owner of a fish cannery. The family lived comfortably in a spacious apartment with big windows on one of the most prominent streets of the city, just a few blocks from the beach.

"We had every modern convenience," Jack said. "Because I lived in the city, I did not realize that many people in Poland were without electricity, indoor plumbing, and telephones.

"Our home was filled with laughter and kisses. My parents were very much in love. They were openly affectionate with each other and with us children. It was a lovely life."

Jack's mother, Cesia *(Sesha)*, dressed elegantly. She wore silk dresses, high heels, jewelry, and hats with veils. In cold weather, she wore her fur coat. She was very beautiful, with dark eyes and long, shiny black hair, which she arranged in the latest styles from Paris.

"Mama was the heart of our home," Jack said. "On winter

Jack has no photo of his mother, but she bore a strong resemblance to her older sister, Tauba Goldwasser, pictured in this photo that survived the war.

Like the boy pictured here in prewar Poland, Jack loved spending a day at the beach. He always went with his mother, sister, and brother.

nights, my mother would warm my comforter on our tile stove and then gently wrap it around me as I climbed into bed. She was an excellent cook and had many specialties. One of my favorites was a sweet fried pastry with pockets of jelly inside. I could never figure out how she got the jelly in there."

Mama took the three children to the market with her, on picnics in the nearby forest, and on outings in the mountains surrounding Gdynia. "We often went to the beach," Jack said. "I remember Papa sometimes taking a break from work to join us. From street vendors, he would buy us handmade waffle cones filled with delicious, rich cream."

The family employed a full-time housekeeper to help with laundry, cleaning, and cooking. Each morning, she arrived early by bus and streetcar from her nearby village to brew the coffee, filling the apartment with its strong aroma.

"She was a pretty, young woman, and I remember how she would lick the red wrapper the coffee came in and then rub it on her cheeks to make it look like she used rouge, which she could not afford," Jack said. "She was good-natured, and I loved to tease her."

Sometimes, Jack also teased Jakob, his brother, who was five years younger than he. Jakob was a handsome little boy and had his mother's jet black hair and dark eyes. Jack felt protective of him and often played with him. Like Jack, Jakob loved sports. Jack often took him to the ice-skating rink and played hockey with him.

Their sister, Jadzia *(Ya-jah)*, was serious and studious. She was three years older than Jack. "Jadzia loved music and listened to Italian opera on the radio while she did her homework," Jack said. "She had perfect penmanship. She was gentle and kind. I remember that she wore little gold earrings with her school uniform, which was a navy blouse with a sailor collar and navy pleated skirt. She had black hair and big hazel-colored eyes."

Like his father, Jack had naturally curly blond hair and blue eyes. "Papa was my hero. I thought he was strong and brave, and I always felt safe with him. I remember the night he brought me a bicycle. It was not my birthday or anything; he just got it for me because he thought I would like it. Even though it was late, I immediately rode it around and around our big mahogany dining-room

Jack's father had sent this photo of himself to a cousin.

table. After that, I rode it everywhere, for I was free to come and go. I even entered bicycle races on Square Kosciuszko—named for the Polish patriot who fought with George Washington in the American Revolution—and once I won third place."

Every school day, before Jack put on his navy blue uniform and walked to his public school, his mother insisted he eat a big breakfast. Typically, it included fruit juice, hot cereal with milk and butter on it, a roll, cheese, and perhaps smoked fish, along with a boiled egg served in a little cup.

"Mama always packed a lunch for me, but after such a breakfast, sometimes I was not hungry, so I would give my food away to some of the poor children who attended our school."

When classes ended, Jack and his friends went to the movies—Charlie Chaplin was Jack's favorite actor—or they played soccer, rode their bikes, or went to see the Greco-Roman-style wrestling matches at the local sports arena. Often they headed to the beach or docks.

"I was a mischievous boy," Jack recalled. "My parents never knew all the things I did that I was not supposed to, especially at the boat docks. The worst was when my friends and I would swim alongside ships in the harbor. It was very dangerous, because you could be crushed between the ship and the dock. This had once happened to a boy. But I never thought about the danger. We would even climb up the ship ladders and then dive into the water. The port police often chased us. I was lucky my parents never found out, or I would have been punished. City boys like me learned to get away with things. We were clever."

Jack's parents frequently entertained friends and relatives, some of whom stayed with the family for weeks at a time. Both parents had come from large families. Jack's father had two brothers and two sisters, and his mother had nine brothers and sisters. Jack did not know his paternal grandfather, who lived in a small town in another part of Poland, but a few relatives lived close by and would gather along with friends at the Mandelbaums' for special occasions.

Jack was especially fond of Uncle Sigmund, his father's younger brother, who was only seventeen when Jack was born. "Uncle Sig looked older than he was because he had lost most of his hair due

An observation tower at the top of one of Danzig's well-known buildings overlooked one of Jack's favorite bridges. Danzig was Jack's birthplace, and his family frequently visited friends and relatives living there.

to a childhood illness," Jack recalled. "He was strong and plump and had rosy cheeks, and I loved it when he visited us, because he was so much fun."

A frequent visitor was Mama's pretty youngest sister, Hinda, who stayed for long periods of time with the family. She was college educated and quite spoiled. She was interested in clothes and makeup and in having a good time with her many boyfriends, all of whom adored her.

Jack's family apartment occupied the entire second floor of this building in Gdynia.

When the Mandelbaums entertained, Jack often eavesdropped. Politics was always a topic. "This is how I learned many things," he said. "Germany was our close neighbor, and I remember the adults talking about the oppression of Germany's Jews. Adolf Hitler, the Nazi dictator of Germany, was making life miserable for them."

One Jewish friend of his father's, Mr. Poncz, a rotund man who was normally cheerful and full of jokes, always got agitated when talking politics. He would pace the room, chomping on his cigar, his face getting very red as he wondered aloud why Hitler hated the Jews so much and why he blamed them for everything wrong in Germany.

"Mr. Poncz talked about his German Jewish friends and their loyalty to everything German," Jack recalled. "Many of his friends fought bravely for Germany in World War I and were very patriotic, yet they had been stripped of their citizenship rights.

"I remember my father replying that while Hitler persecuted other groups, including Communists, Gypsies, and anyone who politically opposed him, he, like many Germans and other Europeans, hated the Jews. This hatred went back to ancient rivalries and misunderstandings over religion and nationality. Hitler made the Jews the scapegoat for Germany's loss of World War I and for its economic problems. He declared in one speech that if there were another war, it would be the Jews' fault and would result in the destruction of the Jewish race in Europe."

Some people resented Jews who had prospered financially. Others distrusted Jews who lived apart, speaking Yiddish—which was the traditional language spoken by Eastern European Jews— and following ancient customs of dress, culture, and education.

Jack's parents were concerned about increasing acts of violence against Polish Jews in other parts of Poland, but they did not speak of these things in front of their children.

"They wanted to protect us," Jack said. "I knew they were worried. At the movies, I saw newsreels of Hitler speaking at huge rallies, and I saw footage of his troops marching into Czechoslovakia. Sometimes, we heard Hitler ranting on our radio. We lived just twelve miles from the German border and spoke German as well as Polish, so we knew what he was saying."

Gdynia, a city of 250,000, had such a small Jewish population that it did not have a synagogue or a rabbi. Ninety percent of Poland's population was Catholic and ten percent was Jewish. Although Jack's parents had both grown up in religious Jewish households, they did not go to weekly services. However, they did observe the major Jewish holidays, such as Passover, and they wanted Jack to have a bar mitzvah, the traditional Jewish coming-of-age ceremony, when he turned thirteen.

That summer of 1939, when he was twelve, Jack's parents engaged a young Jewish scholar to tutor him in study of the Torah and the Hebrew alphabet so he would be prepared for his bar mitzvah. His mother began making the traditional fruit brandy, sealing it in jars to ferment until the celebration.

All of this seemed mysterious to Jack, who believed in God but at that time knew more about the Catholic faith than the Jewish faith. In his public school, nuns and priests taught the Catholic prayers. Jack knew them all by heart. Though Jews did not celebrate Christmas, he would join his Catholic friends in the tradition of carrying manger scenes from house to house while singing Christmas carols.

Even when talk of war with Germany began in earnest, Jack thought of himself as Polish, rather than Jewish. "We were full of patriotism," Jack said. "We knew the Germans hated the Poles and wanted our land. Our attitude was, *Let 'em come! We'll lick 'em in a week.*"

As the summer of 1939 wore on, more and more stories

Hitler salutes his soldiers during a Nazi parade.

surfaced about Hitler's hatred of Jews. Many German Jews tried to leave Germany, but few found places to go. Most countries were anti-Semitic—which meant they were prejudiced against Jews—and would not allow them in. Some countries, like the United States, had strict immigration quotas. Jack overheard his father telling his mother he was worried about what could happen to Jews in Poland, and perhaps they should move to Australia, one country where Jews could still go. But the Australians allowed only one

Several generations of a Jewish family in Poland gathered for this picture, taken prior to the war.

family member to enter the country initially. After six months, if that person had a job and could support the rest of the family, then they could come. Mama refused to consider doing this because of the required separation from Papa.

Jack knew that the year before, when Germany had forcibly expelled many Jewish citizens, dumping them in a no-man's-land between Germany and Poland, Papa had helped them, putting himself at great risk. He secretly brought group after group of these poor people to Gdynia and helped get them safely onto ships that would take them to freedom in other countries—countries that a short time later started restricting immigration. Jack had thought his father very brave to help the German Jews. He felt a thrill go down his spine every time he remembered what his father had done.

Then one day in June, his Hebrew teacher disappeared and Jack's lessons stopped. The lessons had been difficult, and he was relieved he did not have to study anymore.

In August, city officials announced that schools would not open in the fall. Jack was elated. "I thought, Wow! Extra vacation, *and* a war coming. What could be better? My friends and I were thrilled. Every day, we went to the docks to watch naval cadets training on the few ships that were Poland's entire navy."

Though Jack had no way of knowing it, this ended his formal education, both religious and academic.

Compared to Hitler's forces, the Polish military was primitive, consisting of a few airplanes, a few ships, and a small cavalry. Jack's father had served in the army for two years and was clearly worried.

"Papa had a strong foreboding about the war," Jack said.

When rumors began spreading that the Germans were about to start a bombing campaign against Poland, Jack's father feared Gdynia would be a target. He decided that until the danger was past, his wife and children must go stay with his father, who lived in a small town three hundred miles away. He felt they would be safe there.

"But Papa," Jack protested, "you must come, too."

"I will. But for now, I will stay to close up the business and the house," he replied. He held Jack's hands tightly, and Jack never forgot his words. "You are my eldest son. I am counting on you to take care of our family."

2

The day of their departure in mid-August, the train station was jammed with people leaving the city for the safety of the countryside.

Jack's father got Mama and the children settled into a first-class compartment on the train. They each had one suitcase, and Mama carried a basket filled with food for the twelve-hour journey. Papa said he would ready a shipment of clothing, money, and other necessaries and send it along just as soon as he could.

"I will see you within a month," he promised as he kissed each of them good-bye. "There is nothing to worry about."

Jack knew his parents were acting braver than they felt. Mama blinked back tears as she and Papa gave each other a final tender kiss.

Jack waved to his father as the train pulled out of the station. People were pushing and shoving, trying to grab hold of stair

Compared to the cities, villages in Poland were somewhat primitive.

railings to hop on, even as the train began to pick up steam. Later, Jack would wonder how his father had managed to get them first-class tickets on the overcrowded train. The road leaving town was jammed with automobiles and horse-drawn wagons. Was *everybody* trying to leave Gdynia?

But Papa had said not to worry. The Polish military would stop the Nazis. Papa would join the family in a few weeks. In the meantime, Jack was on vacation—*and* riding a train, which was a special treat.

He and Jakob kept their faces pressed to the window, fascinated by the thatched roofs of the simple country cottages and the sight of farmers plowing with horses. They saw Polish troops marching off to fight the Nazis, and they waved wildly to them. When the

The way deeply religious Jews, like the men in the foreground, dressed and wore their hair immediately distinguished them from the general population. They always wore a hat or skullcap in public, which signified their devotion to God.

train passed through small towns and villages, they saw men with beards. Most wore long black coats and hats. Jack knew they were Jews, but he had not realized that many towns and villages had large Jewish populations. He asked Mama if Grandfather would look like these men. She said he would, that he was devoutly religious. He sang the prayers at his synagogue and never missed a service. She also said he had been a widower for a long time but that he had recently remarried.

Grandfather's house as it looks today. His home occupied the two top floors and overlooked the town square. Jack stood on the balcony to watch the Nazis march into town in September 1939.

The next day, Grandfather was waiting for them at the train station in his little town. He looked distinguished with his full white beard and his long coat. When he met Jack, he frowned. "I am shocked to see the day my Jewish grandson goes without a hat," he said sternly. Jack saw his mother's face redden.

As they walked to Grandfather Mandelbaum's house, Jack noticed everything—all the tiny shops and all the Jewish people dressed in black and speaking Yiddish. "Our town of ten thousand people is mostly Jewish," Grandfather told them. "Everyone is friends. We have no trouble."

Jack soon felt at home in Grandfather's comfortable, large house on the edge of the town square. He eagerly explored the Jewish shops and got to know the friendly shopkeepers. His favorites were the two cheerful deaf-mute brothers who ran the barbershop and who loved to clown around. To please Grandfather, he wore a small round skullcap to show he was Jewish. He also went with Grandfather to have his first ritual Jewish bath in preparation for the Sabbath.

Jack's favorite thing to do was to watch his grandfather paint the lettering on signs, which was his profession. "Grandfather was very much an artist, and I was fascinated by this," Jack said.

Along with everyone else in town, Jack cheered the Polish soldiers riding horseback through the streets on their way to the border to protect Poland. Anticipation about the coming war was building to a fever pitch.

Jack's excitement was tempered by his first tastes of anti-Semitism. Perhaps all the adults in the community were friends—or at least acted as if they were. That was not true of the boys Jack's age. They might have a common enemy in the Germans, but the non-Jewish boys constantly taunted and picked on the Jewish boys. Jack had to learn which parts of town it was safe for him to be in without risk of being beaten up by a non-Jewish gang, or, at the very least, called anti-Semitic names.

Hitler and his officers watch their troops march into Poland on September 1, 1939.

On September 1, 1939, two weeks after the family arrived at Grandfather's, the Nazis invaded Poland. Within forty-eight hours, England and France declared war on Germany, and World War II officially began. Within a week, the German army had all but crushed the Polish forces. Several days later, when Jack and everyone else in town first heard the rumble of tanks a few miles away, they dared hope it might be English tanks coming to defend them.

It was the Nazis. As the troops and tanks entered the outskirts of town, most people hid. The streets were deathly quiet. At

Nazis execute a Polish Catholic priest.

Grandfather's house, everyone was staying inside behind closed curtains. Jack could not stand it, and at the last moment he dashed onto the balcony, which overlooked the town square, to watch them come.

"There were tanks, and trucks full of soldiers, and motorcycles with little sidecars. It was thrilling," he said.

Thrill quickly turned to fear. Even though the town did not resist being occupied, the Nazis had a list of prominent citizens, both non-Jewish and Jewish, and immediately arrested them. In many other places, important people who were arrested were then murdered. Hearing this, everyone in town was shocked. They had thought that if they cooperated, the Nazis would not hurt anyone during the occupation, the war would soon be over, and life would be as it was before. Instead, everyone had to be wary of the soldiers occupying their town. Several townspeople were shot when they disobeyed orders.

"The Germans were the enemy and they could kill you, and they did not have to answer to anyone," Jack said. "We were all afraid."

Throughout September and October, Jack's mother worried constantly about Papa. Why had they not heard from him?

"All of Poland was occupied, including Gdynia—which was never bombed, even though everyone had feared it would be," said Jack. "Was Papa okay? And where were all our things, which he'd said he would send?"

Finally, the depot master at the railroad told Jack's mother not to expect the shipment, that the Nazis were seizing everything coming in by rail. At the end of October, a postcard arrived from Jack's father.

"He said he was in the Stutthof concentration camp and was okay and we should not worry about him," Jack recalled. "That was all he wrote. We did not know that he had been forced to write the card. We did not know what a concentration camp was or why he was there or for how long."

Conditions for Polish Jews worsened. In November, two months after the start of the occupation, Jews were ordered to wear the Star of David, the symbol of Judaism, on the front and back of their clothing; they could be shot on sight if they did not. The star had to be yellow. Next came the order that Jewish children could

Forcing Jews to perform menial tasks, such as scrubbing sidewalks, was one way the Nazis humiliated them in public.

no longer attend school, nor could most Jews hold jobs. Grandfather, on the other hand, was busy, for he was ordered to change all the signs in town from Polish to German.

Grandfather and his Jewish friends had assumed that if the Nazis made any move against them, their non-Jewish neighbors would defend them. "Instead, almost all of them shunned us and wanted nothing to do with us," Jack said. "It was not that people were Nazi sympathizers, just that deep down, even if they had not

Jack's grandfather read prayers at this synagogue. After the Jews were deported, Polish residents of the town looted the once-magnificent structure and allowed it to fall into ruins.

realized it before, most of them were anti-Semitic. This was a terrible blow, especially for my grandfather, who had lived in harmony all his life with non-Jews and thought they were his friends. As for me, I considered myself Polish, but now I was identified as a Jew, and I was confused by this."

Everyone, Jewish or not, began to worry about food shortages. Mama had no money—just the few pieces of jewelry she had brought with her. Jack's aunt, who lived in a nearby town, was expecting a baby and wanted Jack's sister, Jadzia, to come help her.

She and her husband owned a flour mill and promised that Jadzia would never go hungry.

"My sister wanted to go," Jack said. "She thought it would make things easier for Mama. Finally, my mother said yes, because she did not want my sister to suffer hunger, but it broke her heart to have Jadzia separated from us."

Soon after Jadzia left, the Nazis set up a border between the two towns. In an instant, the land on Jack's side was now officially part of Germany. His sister's side was still in Nazi-occupied Poland. And travel between the two towns was forbidden.

Distraught, Mama decided in December that they should go stay with her older brother in a nearby village. With her husband and daughter gone, she yearned for the comfort of her own family.

"Somehow, she got word to my uncle, and he said for us to come," Jack said, "but to hurry while travel was still permitted. My grandfather understood my mother's need. I hugged him very tightly and said good-bye."

3

A GROWING FEAR

The uncle was a kind man, and he welcomed his sister and her sons. He had a simple one-story house with a small cellar used to store coal for cooking and heating, and potatoes, the main staple of their diet. He and his wife had five children, and Jack and his mother and brother squeezed in with the family.

Jack and Jakob slept on the floor on a mattress filled with straw. By the second day, they were scratching themselves. "Lice," Jack said. "The mattress was probably full of them. My mother was horrified and scrubbed and scrubbed us, but it was very hard to keep from getting them, because everything in the house was infested. I remember the women in the village inspecting one another's heads for lice. A city boy like me would notice this."

The house had no running water. Everyone used an outdoor latrine. Keeping clean was difficult. "I still remember my uncle

The Nazis used specially trained dogs to help control occupied areas.

taking a mouthful of water from a bucket, spitting it into his hands, and then washing his face with it," Jack said. "I was not comfortable with any of this."

For the first time in Jack's life, food was rationed. His uncle kept all food under lock and key. When dinner came, you got your portion. If you wanted more, too bad.

"I was hungry all the time. So was Jakob. One day, Mama took us to a farmer who gave us thick black bread and tall glasses of buttermilk. To this day, I remember how delicious they tasted."

Jack's beautiful mother was not welcomed by the women in the village, who wore shapeless dresses and hid their hair under scarves. When they saw Mama, elegant in her fine dresses and high heels, they criticized her. "A woman who doesn't even know where her husband is, and *look* at her!" they would say.

"They did not know how deeply she suffered on the inside," Jack said. "She was trying to be strong for my brother and me, but she was terribly worried about my father, my sister, and the rest of her family scattered throughout Poland."

The Nazis continued to lower their net over the Jewish population. Already there was a curfew from dusk to sunup, and Jews caught on the streets could be shot on sight. Jews were no longer allowed to use the library or attend public events. All Poles carried identity cards, and the Nazis stamped the cards of Jewish Poles with a big *J* for *Jude,* which means "Jew."

Then Jews were forbidden to travel. Jack's uncle had a small factory that produced spools of thread, but he could no longer go to a large city for necessary supplies. A Catholic railroad official who was his friend secretly got them for him.

One day, everyone in the village was ordered to gather by a certain large tree. Nazi soldiers kept their guns on the crowd as a military truck pulled up. In the back was the Catholic railroad official.

"Everyone let out a gasp, for we barely recognized him. The

Catholics all crossed themselves," Jack said. "It was horrible. He had been a large, robust man with a big handlebar mustache. We could tell he had been starved and tortured. The Nazis said he was guilty of helping the Polish Resistance. Probably they were trying to get contact names from him, and for a long time afterward, my uncle was fearful he would be arrested, since this man was his friend and had helped him.

"We were forced to watch while they hanged him. His last words were, 'Long live Poland!' Everyone cried. It was the first time I saw someone die, and I had nightmares about it for a long time."

Each week in the town square, the Nazis posted a new edict against Polish Jews, each more extreme than the last. "It's hard to remember them, there were so many. For example, if you met a soldier on the sidewalk, you had to tip your hat and step off the sidewalk into the gutter until he passed," Jack said. "The Nazis created these to make us feel we were second-class."

Jack quickly became expert at avoiding soldiers. You disappeared if you saw them approaching. You did not even want to pass one. If soldiers stopped you and questioned you, the best you could do was stand erect, take your cap off, and keep your head down. No eye contact, ever. And whatever you were asked, you answered.

With so many troubles, Jack turned serious. "I lost my fun-loving attitude about life. I had to be the man in the family and look out for Mama and Jakob," he said. "Adults tried to protect us children from what was happening, but through no fault of their own, they failed us."

A Jew climbing into a truck during a forced labor roundup is kicked by a German soldier, to the delight of other soldiers.

In January 1940, a month after Jack arrived at his uncle's, the Nazis demanded the services of three hundred adults every day to assist with work projects. With just nine hundred Jews in the village, this meant every able-bodied adult male had to work. Since Jack was only twelve, his name was not on the list.

"But there were some well-off people who didn't want to do this labor, and they were willing to pay for someone to take their place," Jack said. "I jumped at the chance. I had been helping out in my uncle's factory, wanting to do my share, so I was learning what hard work was."

The Nazis used Jewish men as forced labor to aid the war effort.

The first day, the forced-labor crew's job was to remove heavy snow from a road. Because they had no snow-removal equipment, this had to be done with shovels. The snow was two feet taller than Jack. As he worked alongside the men, nobody questioned his age. They understood what he was doing.

That night, exhausted but full of pride, he was able to hand his grateful mother the few coins he had been paid.

From then on, six days a week, every minute of daylight, he worked as a substitute. His mother hoarded the little he earned, and after several months, she was able to rent a room for the three of them. "She wanted to get Jakob and me cleaned up," Jack said. "When we moved out of my uncle's home, he was supportive, and he and my mother remained close. Mama paid the rent and fed us by using my earnings and by selling her last pieces of jewelry."

The small room had a bed, a stove, and two chairs. Every morning, Jack rose at five A.M. and reported for work, never knowing where he would be assigned that day. It was always hard labor—digging cisterns, building roads, hauling bricks, crushing rocks. By using forced civilian labor to do these tasks, the Nazis could send more soldiers to the front.

"On our work details, the soldiers were strict with us—they would scream at us and even hit us—but I never saw them shoot anyone, like they did in other places," Jack said.

The war pushed on, and the Nazis won victory after victory. Soon they occupied most of Europe. Jack turned thirteen in April 1940. By the time he turned fourteen in 1941, he had been supporting his mother and brother with his daily labor for two years. He was always ready to work hard. His body got tougher and stronger, and he took pride in how much he could do. Sometimes, he worked in a metal shop. For a while, he worked in a factory.

He never felt sorry for himself. "I knew my mother and brother needed me, and I accepted this responsibility. I never forgot my father's saying he counted on me to take care of our family."

Every night, he returned to the room to have dinner with Mama and Jakob. "We ate whatever Mama could scrounge up," he said.

"Everyone in the village was hungry."

People were running out of money to pay Jack as a substitute, and he made barely enough to keep the family going. He worried about what would happen when he could no longer earn anything. Along with his mother, he worried about his father in the concentration camp and his sister, Jadzia, who was still staying with the aunt and uncle.

Then the Nazis gave him a new worry. Sometimes, they would block off a street, round up healthy Jewish workers, and send them deep into Germany as slave labor. Nobody heard from them again.

"I was getting older and I was afraid this was going to happen to me," Jack said. "I tried to be very careful never to be where they would catch me, but if they decided to block off a street, there would be no escape. I knew if I disappeared, my mother would go crazy. She could not stand to have another family member missing."

Jack had been assigned to assist a Catholic electrician who was rewiring the home of a Nazi official. It was dangerous work, but Jack approached it as he did everything, doing the best job he could.

"I had a good attitude and I knew the electrician liked me," Jack said. "I also knew he was concerned I was going to get assigned to another job. So I took a big risk. I asked him to get me an official letter with a Nazi stamp on it saying that I worked for the Nazis, so I could come back every day to help him. My hope was that if they caught me in a raid and I showed the paper, I would be let go."

The electrician was able to get the letter, and Jack made sure he always had it with him.

Hitler was a charismatic leader who often enthralled audiences at huge rallies.

"Whatever they decided the rules of the game were, I made up my mind to play by them," Jack said. "I just wanted all this over with so that I could get back to the life I had known. I still believed the war would end soon and my sister would return and Papa would come for us."

In June 1941, Hitler invaded the Soviet Union. He also stepped up his war on the Jews. By the end of the year, one section of Jack's village was turned into a restricted living area for Jews. To make room for this ghetto, non-Jewish families were forced to move out of their homes, and three or four Jewish families were moved into each one. Jack and his brother and mother were assigned to one room in a small house.

"This was not as bad as a city ghetto with barbed wire, but we were very crowded and we had little food," Jack said. "We did not know why the Nazis wanted us all together like that."

They would find out soon enough.

4

Jack heard the rumble of trucks at five A.M., just at the moment soldiers beat on the door of the house. He was instantly awake, his heart pounding wildly. It was still dark. What could they want?

"Everybody out! All Jews out!" he heard them shout. Soldiers burst through the front door. They swarmed through the house, their boots stomping on the wooden floors and stairs. Mama was already up and pulling on her clothes when a soldier jerked open the bedroom door. "Out, Jews!" he said roughly. "Five minutes! Out!" The soldier crossed the hall to open another door.

"Jack, Jakob," his mother said urgently, "put on all your clothes. Hurry very quickly."

Jack could hear the fear in her voice. Somewhere in the house, someone screamed. He heard the soldiers shout angrily. They came through the hallway again, this time pushing an old couple in front of them. The man was trying to calm the woman, telling her she must be quiet, but her screams had turned to wailing. "They are going to kill us!" she cried. "I know they are going to kill us!"

A soldier stopped by their door, pointing his gun directly at Jakob. "Out!" he shouted. Almost dressed, Jack reached for his jacket, making sure the letter was in the pocket, then grabbed Jakob's hand and followed Mama through the door. He was afraid the soldier would hit her. Or Jakob. He did not care if he got hit, but Please, he thought, do not hit them.

Outside, in the dim first rays of light, soldiers were ordering people to begin walking to the village square. One man started to run and was shot in the back. A woman fell on the ground, shrieking. Another shot. Jack heard his mother gasp. He hoped Jakob had not seen.

People who had been asleep only fifteen minutes earlier stumbled along the streets. Many were sobbing. Others looked numb with shock. A few prayed out loud. Soldiers barked orders, keeping everyone together.

Jack and his mother and brother held tightly to one another as they were pushed forward. In the confusion, family members became separated. People frantically searched for one another, screaming out names. Babies wailed and children sobbed. The ghetto emptied, and the square quickly filled with people. Jack knew his uncle and his family were somewhere in the crowd.

It was so simple to do this, he thought, because we were all together. Will they shoot all of us?

When the Nazis rounded up the Jews from ghettos for deportation to the camps and gas chambers, they usually did so without warning, terrorizing the populace into cooperating.

Someone broke free of the crowd and ran past the soldiers. Several shots rang out. Cries of horror rose from the crowd. The soldiers pointed their guns menacingly, daring anyone else to try to escape.

"What is happening?" people asked in terror. "Tell us what is happening!"

"They are rounding us all up," a man standing next to Jack's mother said. "They are going to deport us."

In many places, the Nazis rounded up Jewish men, women, and children and executed them, rather than sending them to concentration camps.

Jakob's eyes grew large. "What does that mean?" he whispered to Jack.

"It means they settle you somewhere else. Give you a new home," Jack lied. He tried not to think of the stories he had heard lately of mass killings; of men, women, and children being forced to dig their own graves and then being shot and thrown into them.

"But Papa will not know where we are," Jakob said.

Jack tried to reassure him. "You know our papa. He will find us."

"Whatever happens, do not let go of each other's hands," Mama said over and over. "We must stay together."

The sun rose with the promise of bright warm weather. It was June 14, 1942. Soldiers surrounded them. Though hours passed, no one was allowed to move or go to the bathroom. Everyone was hungry and thirsty. Children cried. Jack wished they could just sit down. His mother was wearing high heels, but she did not complain. Worry etched deep lines in her face. An elderly woman fainted, and before people around her could help her get up, a soldier rushed over and hit her hard with his gun. She lay on the ground, moaning. A shot. Stunned silence was followed by shrieks and cries from the crowd.

Noon came, and then late afternoon. Still they stood. Then, finally, the soldiers began ordering people to line up. Jack and his mother grabbed Jakob's hands. Some of the old people could barely walk after standing for so long. Soldiers were quick to use their gun butts to keep order, striking out at anyone who did not stay in line.

Then they began to move through the streets, every Jewish man, woman, and child from the village, nine hundred people in all. Jack could see faces behind closed curtains, watching. A group of village men stood by a church. He recognized one of his uncle's neighbors, a man who had grown up with Jack's mother and his uncle. "Dirty Jews!" one of the men sneered, spitting on the ground.

Jack touched the letter in his coat pocket, the one with the Nazi stamp on it. Could it somehow help? But help with what? "They are going to shoot us all," a woman said over and over, sobbing. "Where are they taking us?"

Ahead loomed the high brick walls of the local brewery. Inside, Jack knew, was a large grassy area and the buildings where beer was made.

At the gate, everything was chaos. Jack tried to see what was happening. As people were pushed forward by the soldiers, a Nazi officer signaled them to go right or left. Children screamed as they were pulled from their parents. The air was filled with the din of wailing babies and frantic adults, cut by the angry shouts of soldiers.

"We *must* stay together," Mama said urgently, her eyes wide with fear.

What did going left or right mean? Which was better? It looked like the stronger people—those who could work—were going to the right. Jack could not tell. They were hustled forward, Mama and Jack holding tightly to Jakob's hands. Suddenly, it was their turn. Jack thought his heart would thump right out of his chest.

The officer glanced at the three of them and signaled to the left. Rough hands pushed them out of the way.

Summoning all his courage, in one desperate moment, Jack pulled out the letter with the Nazi stamp and thrust it at the officer. "I am an electrician's helper. My mother and brother and I can work." His hands and voice shook. He kept his eyes down, not daring to make eye contact.

The officer skimmed the letter and tossed it aside. He nodded to a soldier. Jack was jerked to the right and pushed into a group of what he now realized was only men. No women and children, no old folks. Horrified, he tried to cross back, but a soldier blocked

These Hungarian Jews have just arrived by boxcar at Auschwitz-Birkenau. Men are being separated from women and children on the selection platform. Prisoners in striped uniforms are assisting the guards.

Jack's way, his gun pointing directly at him. Another soldier pushed him. He could no longer see his mother and brother in the crowd.

His knees buckled. He had promised his father he would take care of them.

"It was the worst moment of my life," Jack said. "It never entered my mind they would take me away from them."

On Jack's side were about one hundred males. Jack was the youngest. Everyone else, including his mother, his brother, and his

With women and children on one side and men on the other, families are forever splintered.

uncle and his family, was on the other side.

Trucks pulled up to the gate. Jack and the others were pushed aboard by the soldiers, who were shouting at them to move forward and to stay silent. Jack was in the middle and could no longer see anyone.

As the trucks pulled out, Jack tried not to panic. Would Mama and Jakob be okay? How would they get along without him? Would he be able to find them?

The trucks rumbled through the village and out into the countryside. In the back of Jack's truck, the terrified men were

During the selection process, a Nazi official determines if a man is strong enough for hard labor. The Jewish woman in the foreground has been selected for labor instead of immediate death.

silent. Jack had no idea where they were going. "But I reasoned that if they were going to shoot us, they would already have done it. They did not have to take us on a truck. Maybe they had a job for us to do and then they would bring us back to our families. I tried to believe that."

When the trucks stopped several hours later, it was already dark. They had driven through heavy iron gates into an open area inside a compound of buildings. Around them were concrete posts strung with electrified barbed wire. Bright searchlights shone down from the guard towers. In the shadows, Jack saw bedraggled men in blue-and-gray-striped uniforms, hurrying from one building to the next. What place was this?

"The tailgates of the trucks were lowered and the guards ordered us to jump down," Jack said. "They began to beat us with rubber truncheons, screaming at us as we stumbled in the glaring light. I tried to protect my head and face as I moved in the direction they pushed us.

"They wanted to terrorize us so we would do what we were told. It worked. From that moment on, I was always afraid."

5

THE RIGHT TO DIE

"We staggered through the blows from the guards," Jack remembered. "They barked at us to line up in rows of five. We stood silent, with our heads down. The officer in charge told us we were now prisoners of Hitler's SS, special forces, and were in the Blechhammer concentration camp, across the border, in Germany. We had no rights. The *only* right we had was to die."

Jack and the others were taken to a room where they were ordered to undress and then form lines. Camp prisoners, who were not allowed to speak to the new prisoners, roughly shaved off all their body hair to help prevent lice. Jack touched his newly shaved scalp. His hair was only three-quarters of an inch long and had a stripe through the middle, shaved right down to the skin, to mark him as a concentration camp prisoner.

Next, he had to stand still while his skin was coated with a chemical disinfectant to kill lice. He had to bite his lip and force himself not to cry out, so badly did the solution burn. Around him, men screamed in pain.

Uniforms were tossed to them, and Jack quickly put his on. It looked like that worn by every other prisoner—coarse cotton with blue and gray stripes. He had no underwear or socks, but at least the uniform had pockets. On the left front was a number: 16013. This meant 16,012 prisoners had been processed into this camp before Jack. From now on, no matter which camp he was in, the number 16013 would be his identification. As far as the Nazis were concerned, he no longer had a name.

"I learned from other prisoners that in some camps they tattooed your number on your arm," Jack said. "However they did it, reducing your identity to a number was part of their way of dehumanizing you."

Once he had the uniform, Jack was issued shoes with wooden bottoms and ankle-high canvas tops. When he tried to take a step, he almost twisted his ankle because he could not bend his foot. How clever of his captors: Escape would be very difficult in these.

Finally, the new prisoners were allowed to use the latrine. They lined up at a shed. It was night now, and there was no light. In the blackness, when it was his turn, Jack found the board with holes in it placed over a pit.

"The flies were thick and the stench was overwhelming," Jack said. "The body odor of other prisoners also was horrible. Everything in this camp stunk and was filthy."

When all the processing was done, Jack was assigned to one of the hundreds of look-alike sleeping barracks. There were row upon row of these long, low wood buildings, each with an aisle through the middle and tiers of wooden bunks. Jack quickly memorized the number above the door so he would always be able to find his.

Prisoners slept on bunks filled with loose straw. Each had a thin blanket but no pillow. "The barracks had no insulation or heat. Since this was June, it did not yet matter," Jack said.

On his bunk was a little metal can to hold food when he had a meal. But that would not be this first night.

"I had just gotten there when the single lightbulb hanging from the ceiling was turned off and we were ordered to be quiet. I lay on my bunk in the dark, trying to understand what had happened to me. I was fifteen years old. My father had been in a Nazi concentration camp for three years, and now I was also in one. My sister was with our uncle and aunt and was okay, as far as we knew. I was sure my mother and brother were all right, but it was going to be very hard for them without me, and I knew Mama would be sick with worry for me.

"Whatever this place was, whatever was going to happen, I vowed I would somehow stay strong and I would get back to them."

6

The light came on in the dark. "Up!" shouted a harsh voice. "Up! Up!"

Jack was instantly awake. Prisoners were hopping down from the upper bunks, grabbing their cans and hurrying out the door. A fat man wearing the same uniform as the prisoners thundered through the barracks, a truncheon in his hand. He was swinging left and right at the men, screaming at them to hurry up. This was the *kapo*, the prisoner in charge of the hundred men in this barracks. Jack could not believe his size. All the other men were skin and bones.

As the kapo reached his bunk, Jack just managed to duck a blow coming his way. Grabbing his can, he started for the door, almost tripping in the awkward wooden shoes. He followed the other prisoners to an outside area where he saw men eating. Already his stomach was growling. He had not eaten in over a day.

Then the smell struck him—something putrid, something so rotten that you would not even throw it into the pigpens back in his uncle's village. For a moment, he thought he would throw up. How could food smell so bad?

The line was long and desperate. Jack fought to hold his place as the prisoners behind him pushed and shoved. They were like starving dogs. The kapos walked along, striking out savagely. Jack could see that you treated them with the same deference you gave the guards. Not all of them were fat like his kapo, but most of them seemed mean. They did the work of overseeing the prisoners, while the guards stood at a distance or stayed up in the watchtowers.

Prisoners received their portions of food and immediately wolfed them down. In spite of the threat of a beating, hands reached out to grab for anything and everything. Jack felt a knot in his stomach as he neared the front of the line. What if someone took his food from him?

Ahead of him, prisoners thrust their cans toward the cook, who filled them. When the prisoner in front of Jack held out his can, the cook eyed him and then put some thin soup from the top of the kettle in it.

"Give me more!" the prisoner protested. "This is just water!"

Instead, the cook struck the prisoner's can with the soup ladle, spilling the watery contents on the muddy ground. With a cry, the prisoner fell to his knees and began to lick up whatever traces of the soup he could find. A kapo was instantly above him, pounding him on the head, shouting at him to get up. Dazed and unable to rise, the man was dragged away by the kapo, who continued to beat him.

Jack's heart beat hard as he held out his can. The cook filled it. To his surprise, Jack saw a potato floating in the thin soup. He glanced at the cook to thank him, but the cook did not look at Jack. Jack quickly stepped away before a kapo could strike him. In this strange new world, one man got nothing and the next got a precious bit of potato in an otherwise-watery soup. What was the secret of getting the potato?

The soup's taste was so disgusting that Jack could barely swallow his first sip. It reeked of rotten turnips, and he could see flecks of dirt in it. At home, he would have thrown it away. But not here. He drank it as quickly as he could.

"You get the bread tonight," a prisoner standing by him said quietly. "Do not try to save it. Someone will steal it."

Jack recognized the man from the bunk next to his.

"Come quickly now," the man said. "You have only a few minutes to put your can on your bunk and get to the latrine. Then it is roll call."

Jack concentrated on not stumbling as they hurried back to the barracks. It was hard to do anything but shuffle in the shoes. He learned the man's name was Aaron and he was a barber from Kraków. He had sunken cheeks and a large nose. He had been in the camp for two months. He did not know where his wife was, but he presumed she must also be in a camp. Fortunately, he said, they had no children.

As they stood in line at the latrine, Aaron pointed to a tall smokestack on the other side of the camp and told Jack it was the crematorium, where corpses were incinerated, leaving only ashes. "It's quicker and more sanitary than burial, and many die here," Aaron said by way of explanation.

Jack shuddered. The Nazis seemed to have figured out everything, including how to eliminate evidence that someone had ever existed.

Finished at the latrine, they hurried toward the open square in the middle of camp and then into a row behind the fat kapo. "Say nothing in line except to call out your number when they count us," Aaron warned. "Stay at perfect attention and *do nothing* to make them notice you."

Prisoners filled the square, thousands of them. The guards in the watchtowers kept their machine guns on them and surveyed them with binoculars. For the next hour, as the sun came up, kapos shouted, "Count off!" at their groups. Jack saw no one younger than he was. He would not be here, either, if it had not been for the letter with the Nazi stamp.

Finally, the fat kapo seemed satisfied with his group and the counting stopped. Still the prisoners stood, the sun beating down on them. Jack needed to go to the latrine. The soup had made him feel sick. He wished he could ask Aaron what they were waiting for, but he knew better than to speak.

From the corner of his eye, he saw a group of SS officers and guards walking to the front. Several of the guards had snarling

Roll call was always a terrifying experience for prisoners.

German shepherd dogs on short leashes. Jack could only imagine what would happen if one of those dogs was set on a prisoner. The kapos reported numbers to the officers. They talked among themselves. Then an officer blew his whistle and, one by one, the columns were marched off to work. Jack felt exhausted—and the day's work had not yet begun.

The fat kapo ordered Jack into a work detail on the left. Aaron went the other way. Soon Jack and about 150 other prisoners were marching toward the forest outside the camp, SS guards on either side of them, ready to strike a prisoner with a gun butt or beat him over the head for the slightest infraction. Jack struggled with the shoes. Be alert to everything, he told himself. *Do not get hit.*

When they finally stopped, he thought he would collapse. He knew they had come at least three miles. Between the long march in the impossible shoes and the scant and awful breakfast, how could they now work all day?

But they did—without breaks, and with no water or food. All day long, using only axes and chains, they pulled out tree stumps to make way for a road.

It was backbreaking labor. In the afternoon, it got so hot that Jack wondered if they would all go mad from thirst. Then a prisoner stumbled, causing a tree stump just coming out of the ground to fall back in place, requiring it to be pulled out again. The guards were instantly on the prisoner, beating him until he was unconscious. When the group finally headed back to camp, two prisoners helped the injured man.

"They will shoot him in a day or two," a prisoner whispered to Jack. "If you cannot work, it is the end of you."

Jack felt his blood chill. He could already see two differing philosophies among the prisoners. Some tried to work as little as possible so they could conserve their energy. Others tried to work harder so they could avoid beatings. The latter was the better way, Jack decided. He would do here what he had done on the labor details back in the village: He would not complain. He would act respectful. He would be likable, cooperative, and as good a worker as he could be. He would make sure his overseers considered him of value.

Though he knew they would never do so, he wanted them to say, We can count on Jack. Or rather, We can count on prisoner 16013.

When they reached the camp, the men lined up for their ration of bread. Jack's body was heavy with fatigue. Every muscle ached, and he longed to lie in his bunk, but he was desperate for food. Once again, hunger turned the men into savages. When he was finally given his slice of bread, Jack held it tightly in his hands so no one could grab it from him.

He almost choked on the first bite. He forced himself to eat, wondering what was wrong with the bread. Why was it so gritty? He finished it and hurried to the latrine, holding his nose to avoid the stench.

When he crawled onto his mattress, Aaron was in the bunk next to him. "Where were you today?" Jack asked.

"Except on days when I shave new prisoners, I cut the hair of SS officers and guards and and give them shaves," he said. "It is not so difficult, but if they do not like what I do, they can kill me. If they like it, they might reward me. And you, Jack, you survived your first day?"

"I have never worked so hard—or eaten so little. The bread . . ."

"Full of sawdust."

Jack wondered if he had heard correctly.

"They use sawdust as filler. That is why it tastes so terrible."

"Always?"

Aaron sighed. "The food will not get better. This is all they give you." He made sure no one was watching, then slipped Jack a thick biscuit. "One of the officers liked his haircut today."

"I cannot take your food," Jack replied, though his mouth was already watering.

"He gave me two, and I have eaten one. Take food when you can get it and never question. Many men starve to death here."

Jack nodded in gratitude.

"Get up early to shower. You must try to stay clean, or you will get sick. Tomorrow, I will wake you, but you will learn to wake early on your own," Aaron said.

The fat kapo came through the barracks, his truncheon at the ready. "No talking!" he growled. A minute later, when the lone lightbulb went out, Jack ate the biscuit. His body hurt, yet tomorrow he had to do again what he had done today. Could he? He knew he must.

He closed his eyes and fell asleep instantly.

7

THE GAME

He awoke the next morning covered with lice. Wherever he normally had hair, they were burrowing into his skin and making him itch. He checked his blanket and found it was infested.

He hurried with Aaron to the showers. They stood in a long line. Finally, they reached the dribbles of water from a spigot that passed for a shower. The whole time, they were harassed by kapos to hurry along. Aaron showed Jack how to rinse out his uniform quickly. It felt clammy on his skin and dried stiff. He shuddered, thinking what it would feel like to do this in winter, when it was cold.

But lice carried disease. He had to stay as clean as he could. There was sickness in the camp. Men coughed and had stomach problems. He heard rumors of typhus and dysentery in other camps. Both diseases caused much misery and could be fatal. What if they spread here?

As days became weeks, he grew more sure of the camp routine. Get your share of food, work hard, stay well, stay as clean as possible, avoid beatings. That last one sometimes seemed impossible.

Who could say how or why a prisoner was singled out by the kapos and guards? Blows were random, unexpected, and undeserved: a rubber truncheon across the back, a gun butt to the ribs, a kick in the rear or the stomach. It happened all the time. Maybe you stepped out of line, or maybe the kapo did not like you. They could curse you, take your food from you, or beat you to death. No one stopped them. For every dead prisoner, there were a dozen to take his place.

"You did not expect a guard to do a kindness for you—that almost never happened," recalled Jack. "The best you could hope for was one who did not beat you or have his dog attack you just for amusement."

Somehow, Hitler and the Nazi SS who ran the concentration camps had convinced the German guards that Jewish prisoners were subhumans and that all prisoners, Jewish or not, deserved this brutish treatment. Jack knew the guards believed these things, for they said so often enough to the prisoners. There was no arguing with them. You would get your head bashed in for that.

The kapos were another story. All of them were prisoners, some Jewish. Kapos wore special armbands to identify them. The kapos in the different barracks had special privileges and could steal food before it reached the prisoners. The fat kapo did it all the time. Other kapos were in charge of the work details. In all, there was perhaps one kapo for every fifty prisoners. Jack learned that most kapos had been in German prisons before the war for such crimes as murder or theft. When the SS set up its vast system of concentration camps, they moved these criminals into the camps to help control the prisoners.

Some kapos were insane, some were sadistic, and some were not so bad. It would have been easy to despise them, since they had extra food and privileges and had power over the prisoners, but Jack knew their lives were hard, too: They stayed alive only as long as they followed orders.

Jack chose not to hate them or the guards and officers. Hate was destructive and served no good. To hate would consume his strength. Everyone in this camp, he reasoned, had been caught up by events in the war. Everyone had a role to play. To conserve energy, he had to stay as positive as possible—and hate was a negative emotion.

Each non-Jewish prisoner had a colored triangle by his number to denote his "crime." The fat kapo's was green, meaning he was a professional criminal. Jack was sure he was a murderer. Another prisoner in his barracks had a red triangle, so he was a political prisoner who had opposed Hitler. Gypsies wore black. Homosexuals wore pink triangles. Purple was for non-Jewish religious prisoners, such as the Seventh-Day Adventists, or Protestant or Catholic church leaders who opposed Hitler.

A large majority of the prisoners were Jewish. In some camps, but not all, they wore a yellow triangle. They were at the bottom of the prison hierarchy. By Hitler's definition, you were Jewish if you had at least one Jewish grandparent. "You were Jewish even if you had converted to Christianity. Even if you had never been in a synagogue in your life. We were a 'race' in Hitler's eyes, and belonging to it was a crime," Jack said.

One night, a few minutes before lights out, an older prisoner named Moshe, who had been in four different camps in three years, stopped by Jack's bunk to visit, as he often did. Moshe had sad eyes and a raspy voice. He had been transported to his first camp in a boxcar in which many people had died of suffocation. Jack assumed that Moshe liked to talk to him because he was young, for Moshe had been a schoolteacher and enjoyed teaching. Jack always listened politely to whatever was on Moshe's mind. That night, it was about how the concentration camps were run.

"You probably think all we do is repair bridges and the like so German soldiers are freed up to fight at the front. But do you know that the camps are also a business?" he asked Jack. "All the able-bodied German men have been drafted into the army, leaving only women to work in the factories. So the SS leases us to them. The SS gets rich and we are worked as slaves. Conditions in those factories are terrible. I know. I have worked in them.

"But not everyone who is Jewish can work," Moshe continued, "and so what does Hitler do with them?" He lowered his voice. "I hear stories—who knows if they are true—that in some places masses of people are taken straight to killing camps rather than to work camps like this. Here they kill you slowly with backbreaking

Some children were imprisoned in the camps, like these Polish children at Auschwitz, before they were sent to the gas chambers.

labor and nothing to eat. But in these special camps, the people are told they are going to take a shower, and many of them are crammed into huge sealed rooms. Then they are gassed to death and their bodies taken to the crematorium."

Jack did not believe him. "Why would they do that? It makes no sense."

Moshe shrugged. "We are Jewish. Hitler wants us all dead. I think it is true."

Later, Jack shared this with Aaron. "I have heard all those rumors, and you should pay them no attention," he said. "Not even the Nazis are *that* inhuman. If the Nazis want us all dead, they are already doing that. Did you try to survive in a ghetto? In the ghetto in my town, they starved us. Whole families died. When I shave new prisoners, I see so many who will not last here more than a few weeks. It is not just because they are weak and will not be able to do the work. It is also because, unless they have been in ghettos, they do not know how to live without their freedom."

"You must feel very sorry for them," Jack said.

"No."

"But they are fellow sufferers," Jack argued. "Surely you feel sympathy for them."

"Jack," Aaron said firmly, "this is a place of endless sorrow. Think only of yourself and those closest to you. If you allow yourself to feel emotion, you will die quickly."

But Jack constantly struggled with his feelings. Most of the men around him were slowly starving to death. They were filthy and sick. Some muttered to themselves. Some cried for their wives and children. They cursed the SS, the Nazis, Hitler, and God.

Yet others, like Aaron, stayed strong and helped others whenever they could. Sometimes, Aaron could get extra food, and he did not have to do heavy outside labor, but his survival depended on something more than that. What was the secret of staying strong?

One day as Aaron cut Jack's hair, he told him. "Think of this as a game, Jack. Above all else, do not take personally what is happening to you. Play the game right and you might outlast the Nazis."

Play the game, thought Jack. He had done that very thing back in his uncle's village. *Find extra food so you do not starve to death.* When you walk across a field, keep your eyes open for a potato, a carrot, for anything edible.

Jack had learned other rules as well. *Do what you are told. Never call attention to yourself. Help your friends,* because you cannot survive without them. *Stay healthy.* Each morning after drinking the thin soup, do what you can to clean up, though you have only a trickle of water, no soap, no towel, no scissors, no toothbrush. If you have a toothache, either learn to tolerate the pain or pull the tooth. See the barbers for monthly haircuts and endure the torture of periodic disinfecting to kill lice, even though you will soon have them again.

It is a game. Think of it that way.

But the consequence for a false move is death.

If you showed up for roll call with so much as a bandage on, you could be ordered aside and later killed. If you were beaten for any reason and could not work, then you would be killed. *But do not take it personally.*

After six months in the Blechhammer concentration camp, Jack was thin but still healthy. He had learned to tolerate lice. No matter how cold and unpleasant it might be, he rinsed his uniform whenever he could. With Aaron's help, he was not starving. At times he was so hungry he ate bark from trees and mushrooms from the forest, though he knew they could be poisonous.

Then one cold winter morning after roll call, Jack and several hundred other prisoners were held back while the others were marched off to work. Without explanation, they were loaded on trucks and driven away from the camp. Jack thought he would

Those who survived the selection process, like these women newly arrived at Auschwitz, had their heads shaven and were issued uniforms.

freeze as the wind whipped around him. It was a snowy day— *February*, someone said; *the year 1943*, someone else said. Word went around that they were being moved to a different camp.

It was true. Hours later, they were processed into the new camp. Jack was filled with anxiety. "As awful as Blechhammer had been, I knew what to expect. Now I had to start over in a new place, and Aaron was not there to help me."

Most of the prisoners in this camp, like the last one, were Polish, German, or Russian. The SS guards, as always, were German. Jewish prisoners who spoke Yiddish could understand enough German because of similarities in the languages. Most Poles already knew German; the Russians quickly learned what they needed to know.

In this camp, instead of having individual bunks in the endless rows of numbered barracks, eight prisoners had to crowd together at night on each of the eight-foot-wide three-tiered wooden platforms that lined the walls. There were no mattresses.

"At least all those bodies provided a little body heat, because the nights could get very cold and our wooden barracks were unheated," Jack said. "If you had to go to the bathroom in the night, you used your food can. The toilets were outside in the open, in the freezing cold. If you were caught in the beam of the searchlight on the guard tower, a guard would try to shoot you. So you used your can, and in the morning you dumped the can, then used it for your soup. You had no choice."

The food was as bad as in the last camp. But here there were no showers, no way to stay clean or to rinse out uniforms. When typhus broke out in the camp, it quickly spread. Jack caught it and had fever, chills, and a terrible cough. He dragged himself to roll call and, using all his strength and determination, continued to work. Many prisoners, including some in his barracks, became delirious and died. Each morning, the dead were carried out, and by night new prisoners were in their places on the platforms. Black smoke belched from the camp crematorium for hours every day.

It took Jack a long time to feel he was over the illness. Other prisoners said he was lucky and would never get it again—that a mild case was like an inoculation.

He was still in the game. He wished he could tell Aaron.

8

HOUR BY HOUR

Though Jack tried not to think about his family, thoughts of them sometimes sneaked up on him. His eyes instantly filled with tears. Papa, Mama, Jadzia, Jakob. How he missed them! He willed himself to picture each one of them in safety and comfort. Papa was in a camp, yes, but perhaps he was a tailor there and worked in a warm place inside. Mama and Jakob were with his uncle back in the village, and his sister had managed to join them.

After the war was over, everyone would return to the beautiful apartment in Gdynia. All their friends and relatives would come again for large gatherings, including Grandfather. Jack would hold his hand as they walked along the beach and watched the ships coming into port. At dinner, there would be so much food they could not even think of eating it all. And never again would they be hungry.

Then Jack would snap back to reality, his stomach almost turning inside out from hunger, his body infested with lice, men around him dying from hunger, disease, and sorrow.

"We tried to help one another," he said, "but people disappeared so fast. They would be transferred to another camp, or they died. You could tell a week ahead who would die. They would get a sort of frozen look on their faces, and we knew they did not want to live any longer. As strange as it sounds, we got used to death because we saw so much of it. It took me a long time, but I learned to think of the dead as fortunate because they were no longer suffering. I hoped Aaron and Moshe and the other men I had known in the first camp were still alive, but I would never be able to find this out."

Jack lost track of passing days. By watching the seasons, he knew he had been in captivity almost a year. He had become sixteen when winter turned to spring in 1943, but he had no way of knowing which day was his actual birthday.

"In a concentration camp, you could think only of staying alive," Jack said. "Every day, every hour was a new challenge. You had to be constantly alert, and protect and care for yourself the best you could. You were always on the lookout for a scrap of food. It was very stressful. The only relevance weather had for us was what obstacles it presented. Were we freezing, wet, or suffocating from heat? We were always hungry and exhausted— that never changed. We had no knowledge about the war or who was winning or losing. The guards told us nothing."

From the guard towers surrounding the camps, guards could keep careful watch on prisoners.

Rumors were part of daily life. Prisoners lived on them. Rumors about the war, rumors about upcoming "selections," when SS officers would weed out the weakest prisoners and ship them off somewhere. Rumors about transfers to other camps.

"Each day," Jack said, "you wondered, *How do I get assigned to less difficult work? How do I make contact with a civilian on a work detail who will slip me a piece of bread from time to time?*"

In a short space of time, Jack was moved twice to other camps. "They took us where they needed us to work," he said. "The camps were different, yet alike. Same overcrowded barracks, each with a

Some of the concentration camps, including Gross-Rosen, had the ironic words "Work Makes One Free" above their entrances.

number. Same food—thin soup, bad bread—same rules, same lice, same filth. Same guard towers with searchlights where guards watched you with binoculars, their machine guns at the ready. Always a crematorium with its black smoke. You went to bed in the dark and awoke in the dark and were counted in the dark so you would be ready to work when it was light. They beat you for any tiny thing."

One of the worst camps Jack was in was called Gross-Rosen. He and the other prisoners arrived late at night. No barracks space was available for them. They were ordered to sleep on a cold concrete floor with no pillows or blankets.

"We were so crowded, we were forced to lie on our sides. If one

The quarry at Gross-Rosen concentration camp is now filled with water. When Jack was there, many prisoners died because of brutal working conditions. Many others committed suicide by hurling themselves off a ledge into the pit of the quarry.

person turned, we all had to turn. But even in *this* circumstance, sleeping was not a problem. Not ever. We could have slept standing up," Jack said.

The camp had a granite quarry, where many prisoners lost their lives. While carrying heavy pieces of granite up the steep sides, they could slip and plunge to their deaths. "Every week, at least a dozen prisoners committed suicide by hurling themselves into the pit," Jack said. "Fortunately, I was only in that camp a short time. Conditions were brutal, and I saw many terrible things there."

Because Jack worked hard and did not complain, he escaped the worst wrath of kapos and guards, though he received an occasional kick or blow like everyone else. Going out of his way to get along sometimes paid off. In one camp, instead of food being served in a central outside location, the soup was carried from barracks to barracks in a large kettle. Jack was selected to help carry the heavy kettle—a dangerous job because of its weight and hot contents. But for his efforts, he was usually given an extra bowl of soup from the very bottom of the kettle, where it was thickest.

One time, he was assigned to help build a sand bed for a railroad. Working around him were civilians who were on forced-labor details, just as he had been back in his uncle's village.

"They still had enough to eat, and I would beg for bread or they would slip some to me without my asking," Jack said. "This lasted only a couple of months, but it helped me keep going. If it was more than a scrap of food, I shared it with other prisoners. They did the same with me."

Surviving the work assigned him was another challenge. One of Jack's jobs was at a chemical plant. He helped load and unload chemicals into railroad cars. Sometimes, he worked inside the plant. "Civilian workers had masks and gloves to protect them from the chemicals, but we prisoners had no protection," Jack said.

Prisoners worked every day on labor details. When they could no longer work, they were killed. Many starved to death or died of disease.

"The fumes were very strong and burned our eyes and throats. If I had stayed there long, I believe the chemicals would have permanently damaged my lungs and eyes."

Another of his jobs was to unload cement bags from railroad cars. Guards with their vicious German shepherds stood over the prisoners. The boxcar was about four feet off the ground, and prisoners had to walk down a shaky wooden plank with a bag as heavy as a man on their shoulders. If you fell off the plank and dropped the bag, it would split open, making a mess. Then the dogs would instantly be on you.

"Going down that plank was very scary, but I remembered how I used to dive from ships in the harbor of Gdynia," said Jack. "That was scary, too, but it was *fun*. So I pretended this was a boyhood game, and I never fell."

Prisoners always watched for opportunities to help themselves. The thickly padded empty cement bags had special value. They could be made into vests if you tore out holes for your head and arms, and they would help block wind and cold and keep you from freezing in the winter when you were working outside and had on only a thin uniform.

"Doing this hurt nothing, yet it was forbidden," Jack said. "Some of us did it anyway. One of our guards carried a bamboo stick and would strike us across the back to see if we were wearing the cement-bag vests. If so, we were punished. But I was never caught."

The worst part of the day was roll call. Not only did it mean standing at attention for hours on end, but it was also when prisoners were punished for some slight infraction, or simply terrorized at random. Everyone was forced to watch when a prisoner was beaten, whipped, shot, hanged, or torn apart by the dogs.

In one camp, six Russian prisoners of war managed to escape, but they were caught later on. Their bullet-riddled bodies were dumped in the middle of the parade ground, and the prisoners had to march around them.

This guard tower and the electrified barbed-wire fence at Auschwitz were typical of towers and fences at all the concentration and labor camps. But there is grass in this photo. Had there been any during the war, the prisoners would have eaten it.

"We were warned this would happen to us if we tried to escape," Jack said. "Every single one of us fantasized about escaping, but to where? All of Europe was occupied by the Nazis. There was no safe place for anyone Jewish. The Russians had a homeland to return to. We Jews did not."

What also kept many from trying to escape was knowing that even if they succeeded, many fellow prisoners would be killed in retribution. "The Nazis terrorized us into doing what they wanted," Jack said. "In photos, you can see the dirt and the starving skeletons of prisoners in the concentration camps, but you cannot smell the fear. Fear is so devastating. To survive the Nazi death camps, you had to be very clever and very lucky."

Jack was determined to survive. "I believed my family was waiting for me. When this was over, they would be there, outside the camp, to greet me. And I would have beaten Hitler at his game."

9

DEATH'S DOOR

Jack awoke one night with pain in his lower abdomen so terrible, he had to bite his tongue not to cry out. He rolled on his back, sweat pouring off him, his insides burning. He had to get to a toilet *now*.

He made it out the door of the barracks, but then he could move no farther. Diarrhea. In the moonlight, he could see the blood in it.

"Oh no!" he whispered, sobs rising in his throat. "Not this!"

He knew it was dysentery, a disease of the intestinal tract that causes bloody diarrhea. Men in the camp were dying of it. Shaking and unable to stand, he crawled back to his sleeping platform. He was desperately thirsty, his bowels on fire. Would he die?

"I could not get up in the morning," Jack recalled. "I lay there moaning, feverish and chilled at the same time. The kapo stopped by me. He was tall, with very dark eyes. He was not a bad man.

Perhaps he even liked me some, for I had always been pleasant to him, the same as I was to everybody. 'You must get up,' he said.

"But I could not stand by myself. He helped me, and, to my amazement, he took me to a sick barracks. I had not known there was such a thing in this camp."

Inside the barracks were cots. The stench in the room made Jack gag. A prisoner doctor looked at him and confirmed that he had dysentery. There was no medicine. A prisoner assisting the doctor gave Jack a bitter solution of coal ground up with water to drink. "It will help," he whispered. Jack forced himself to drink it.

All around him, men moaned in agony. In the corner was a pot where they relieved themselves. Jack fell asleep and slept for a long time, then awoke, delirious. Through blurred vision, he saw two prisoners removing the body of the man on his left, who had just died.

He was given more of the coal solution. Whenever a bed emptied because someone died, a new patient quickly took it.

Jack drifted in and out of a stupor, first awake, then asleep. When he was awake, he made himself drink the bitter solution.

On the third day, so many sick prisoners were being brought in that they were lying on the floor. Jack felt a little better, but he was very weak.

Though his vision was still cloudy, he could see the doctor going from cot to cot, giving the sick men shots. As Jack watched, he realized that within minutes of receiving a shot, the man would jerk spasmodically—and then die. The doctor was killing them!

The work assigned women could be just as difficult as that assigned men.

Prisoners followed behind the doctor, removing the dead bodies, and another ill man would immediately take the newly vacated cot. Soon the doctor would reach Jack.

He tried to sit up, his head woozy. With great deliberation, he put his feet on the floor and stood up. If he fainted, the doctor, the needle . . . He took a step toward the door, then another step, and sank to his knees, almost falling on a man lying on the floor. He worked his way through the sick men, sometimes crawling on his hands and knees.

By the door, he forced himself to stand again. He took several steps and was outside. His heart raced with fear. He had to get back to his barracks. What if a guard in one of the towers saw him and decided to shoot him? He made his way along the barracks, staying in the shadows. A prisoner on an errand saw him and stopped. All he said was "Which barracks?" as though he knew exactly what was happening. Jack told him the number, and within minutes he was on his sleeping platform. The tall kapo said nothing.

The next morning, prisoner 16013 was at roll call, weak and unsteady, but there. That day and for several thereafter, the kapo got Jack assigned to a coveted indoor job in the camp machine shop so he would not have to march outside or do heavy labor. Soon he had recovered.

Together, he and the kapo had cheated Hitler of one more dead Jew.

10

Sometime in the fall of 1943, Jack was transferred again. Like all the other camps he had been in, this latest one was in Germany. He stood in line to get a haircut, weary with fatigue. Out of the corner of his eye, he saw someone approaching him. He was surprised to see it was a boy as young as he was. Even though the boy's head was shaved, Jack could tell he had bright red hair to go with his freckles and blue eyes.

"My name is Moniek (*MOAN-yek*)," the boy said in Polish. He smiled. "Do you have a name, prisoner 16013?"

Jack looked at him warily. No one smiled in camp, and only rarely did they exchange names. But he liked Moniek's friendliness and was pleased he was Polish. "Yes, prisoner 13863," he responded, looking at Moniek's number. "The name is Jack."

A guard walked past them, his chest thrust out. Moniek glanced at the guard in the tower, made sure he was not watching, then thrust out his own chest in hilarious imitation. Jack laughed, surprised by the sound. When had he last laughed?

Moniek filled Jack in on the way the camp operated, which guards were sadistic and which ones were not so bad. By the time they reached the front of the line, Jack knew that Moniek was from the town of Wolbrom in southern Poland. He had been in the camps since 1940—over three years now, and almost twice as long as Jack. He was eighteen—a little over a year older than Jack. Like Mama, Jakob, and Jack, Moniek had first been put into a ghetto. When the Nazis deported the Jews, Moniek had been separated from his parents, two brothers, and two sisters. Like Jack, he was determined to be reunited with his family after the war.

Also like Jack, he had already been in a series of camps. Sometimes, though not in this one, he had worked as a carpenter, a skill for which he had no training.

"When I came into one camp, I met some guys from my hometown. They told me a carpenter had just died, and they said that when it was announced at roll call that a carpenter was needed, I should step forward, because that work was easier than other things. So I did." Moniek winked at Jack and lowered his voice to a whisper. "I knew nothing about carpentry, but I caught on fast enough that the *dummkopf* SS never knew the difference. Work less and conserve energy. That way, you'll live a long life."

Jack had always done the opposite: He worked hard. Lately, he no longer thought it was possible to live a long life. No Jew could survive Hitler. New prisoners told tales of mass slaughter. Everyone now knew that the stories of the gas chambers were true. Because the camps were overflowing with prisoners, the officers held more frequent selections, weeding out the weaker men, who would be taken to the gas chambers and from there to the crematoriums, both of which were now operating in most camps.

All these horrors weighed heavily on Jack. He wondered how God could allow these atrocities to happen. But Moniek refused to dwell on such things. "Better not to think about it, Jack. If you question why, you will not survive this. Think only of this moment and the future," he said as he shared a small piece of bread from his pocket. "There is always reason to hope."

The next morning, they lined up together at roll call so they would be sent on the same work detail. That evening, they waited in the food line together. The food here was as awful as everywhere else, but with Moniek around, even this seemed more bearable. He was always clowning around. He had a smile and joke for every occasion. To Jack's amazement, even when the guards overheard him, they did nothing. Once, he even saw a guard smile at something Moniek did.

"You are too serious, Jack," Moniek would often tell him. And then he would do something to make Jack laugh. Gradually, Jack felt his mood of despair lift. Moniek could actually make him feel lighthearted, and it was helping him.

One cold day, the two boys were ordered to scrub the floor of the SS food-supply shed. A guard took them in and stood over them with a gun. Jack looked around the shed with wonder. It was like a treasure vault. On the shelves were one-pound blocks of butter tightly wrapped in protective paper, and rows of marmalade jars.

He could feel Moniek's excitement, though they dared not speak. Of course they had to try to steal something—they were starving, after all—and the SS would never miss the little they could take. But if they were caught . . .

"I quickly reasoned that more than food was at stake here," Jack said. "They had stolen so much from us—our homes and families, our very identities. To take something from them gave us strength."

As they started to scrub the black slate floor, Moniek communicated through gestures that he had a plan. Using his eyes and covertly pointing with his fingers, he let Jack know he would distract the guard while Jack grabbed something and slipped it into the bucket, where it would be hidden by the scrub rag in the murky water. Jack nodded. He hoped he was brave enough to go through with it.

On signal, Moniek asked the guard where they should empty their buckets and get fresh water. As the guard turned to point to the outside pump, Jack slipped a pound of wrapped butter into his bucket. He knew if he accidentally dropped the bucket, he would be shot on the spot. Carefully, he picked up the bucket and went outside. So far so good. He was not visible from the guard tower.

He frantically looked around for a hiding place and spotted an opening in a stack of wood. He hurriedly slipped the butter in and moved the wood so the butter would not show. Back inside, he used gestures to let Moniek know where the hiding place was.

A short time later Moniek took his bucket out—with a jar of marmalade in it. That night before lights-out, they sneaked back and retrieved the butter and jam. The next morning they shared these wonderful treats with several friends as they ate their daily ration of sawdust-filled bread.

"Was this worth risking our lives for? Perhaps not," Jack said, recalling that incident. "But we would try anything to get food. You could not stay alive on what they fed you. By the beginning of 1944, conditions in the camps got even worse. Moniek and I were starving, just like everyone else."

Once again, Jack's April birthday passed unnoticed. He was now seventeen. Rumors were rampant in the camps that American troops were gaining ground in Europe. In May 1944, Hitler ordered that all Jews in Hungary be deported to the camps, crowding them so much that conditions became even more intolerable. Prisoners died of disease and starvation in ever-greater numbers. The crematoriums operated around the clock. Selections during roll call to eliminate the weakest and most unhealthy prisoners became even more frequent.

"We would stuff paper in our mouths and rub our cheeks to look more healthy," said Jack. "I thought back to how our young housekeeper in our apartment in Gdynia had rubbed her cheeks with red paper to look pretty. Now I tried to make my cheeks red so I could live another day."

When hundreds of thousands of Hungarians were deported into the concentration camps, many were very overcrowded.

Both Jack and Moniek were growing weaker. On work detail, they stayed constantly alert, watching for anything edible they could slip into their pockets and then share that night. "You never saw grass in a concentration camp, because the prisoners ate it," Jack said.

Moniek was assigned to help repair the kennels while the dogs so feared by the prisoners were out on patrol. He found a dog biscuit and a couple of bones in one of the empty kennels. "We dined well that night," Moniek remembered.

With so many prisoners dying, disposal of bodies was a big problem. Jack and Moniek were briefly in a camp that had no crematorium. They were assigned to a one-day work detail to load corpses onto a truck, then throw them off the truck into a common grave outside the camp. The boys tried not to look at the faces. Most of the men had died of starvation. Their mouths were frozen in an expression of horror, and even teenagers looked like old men.

Moniek had no jokes that day. For Jack, the experience was a low point. "I suddenly thought, Who is going to throw *me* off that truck? I did not share this even with Moniek. Deep down, I had always believed I would somehow survive. But on this day . . .

"And you know, that was not even the worst job I ever had. The worst was the time I had to stand in a ditch filled with icy water to my waist. We were supposed to make the ditch deeper. Day after day, we stood there in that freezing mess, with no underwear, socks, coats, or gloves, sleet falling on us, trying to dig out heavy, water-soaked dirt. *That* was the worst work.

"When I was throwing those bodies off the truck, I knew their suffering, at least, was over. At that moment, I felt they were the lucky ones."

11

THE MIRACLE

Every morning, Jack woke up starving. "It is almost impossible to describe this hunger that consumed us," Jack said. "It was a pain in the stomach so severe, it altered the mind. We could not think or talk of anything but food."

Food. Prisoners would say that if once—*just once*—they could feel full, then they could die happy. Moniek's fantasy was to have a whole loaf of bread all to himself. "When I am a free man," he would say, his eyes twinkling with anticipation, "I will have a big round of the best bread and I will cut it up piece by piece and eat it just as slow or fast as I want."

Jack's fantasy was much more elaborate:

My perfect meal, prepared by my mother, of course, begins with rich chicken soup brimming with fat handmade noodles. This is followed by succulent roast duck, all you can eat. There are so many side dishes, you can hardly count them—potatoes of all kinds, and cabbage and every other vegetable, and delicious breads. By then, we have eaten so much, we are in a daze, but we finish with some delicious apple strudel and a glass of lemonade made from real lemons.

As his stomach ached from hunger, Jack's memories were of wonderful family dinners, when his mother would beg him and his sister and brother to eat more, even though they were already stuffed.

When his reveries ended, he was still in a filthy, threadbare, lice-infested uniform in a miserable camp crowded with starving and dying prisoners. Each day, prisoners got the thin soup and the foul bread, but portions grew smaller and smaller.

Typhus was taking many lives. Moniek worried he would catch it, because he had never had it. Jack's fear was not typhus, since he had already had a light case, but starvation. Either he would actually starve to death or become so weak that he could no longer work, and then he would be shipped to the gas chambers.

At some point the prisoners knew 1944 had become 1945. That winter was the worst yet. Jack and Moniek were taken by truck with other prisoners to various places to help clear the rubble left from Allied bombing raids over Germany. All day long they removed debris from destroyed buildings. The few civilians they saw in the distance seemed dejected and hungry and paid no attention to the prisoners.

Did the bombings by the combined forces of France, England, Russia, and the United States mean Hitler was losing? Camp rumors were insistent that Hitler's government was starting to collapse and Russian troops were moving toward Germany. Even if this was true, would they arrive in time to save anybody inside the camps?

Jack could feel his strength ebbing away. He did not know his weight, though he knew it was well under one hundred pounds. He had been lean since the early days of the war, but now he was emaciated—so thin that his bones stuck out and his face looked craggy and old. It would take a miracle for him to survive much longer, and miracles were in short supply in the concentration camps.

Then one occurred.

First, Jack and Moniek were ordered to report to a storage room next to the kitchen to peel potatoes for the guards' soup. With an SS guard standing over them, they peeled all day long. The dirty discarded peelings were put in the prisoners' soup. As Jack and Moniek worked, each managed to make a few peels extra thick, so they contained some potato, and then slip these into their pockets to eat later. Even this tiny bit of nourishment, they knew, would help them stay alive a little longer.

They worked hard and tried to be cooperative and likable. Moniek was soon telling jokes, determined to get the guard to smile. Each day, it was the same guard. Like all guards, he acted stern and unfriendly and often threatened to beat them if they did not work faster.

But he never hit them, nor did he ever tell Moniek to shut up.

And then one day, after several weeks of peeling potatoes—weeks they were grateful to have the peelings and not to be working outside in the freezing cold—they reported for work and were told by this guard that the cook and his helper had come down with typhus. Jack and Moniek, he said, must take over the cooking.

"We could only stare at him in astonishment," recalled Jack. "Had he gotten us this job? But he would not look at us, and we did not see him after that."

Being a cook was the most valued job in the camp. As long as there was any food at all, bad as it was, the cooks would not starve. You did not need to know *how* to cook. All you did was boil water and vegetables together to make the thin soup.

The boys immediately moved into the kitchen, fearful that if they were not there every moment, someone would take over their jobs. The kitchen was a big room, and it was warm. In the center were three huge kettles, each four feet tall, hung over beds of hot coals. Soup ingredients were whatever had been scrounged up: turnips, potatoes, beets, spinach. The boys were not allowed to wash or peel these items or even to cut off rotten parts. The spinach was full of sand.

"It felt like grit in your teeth. The soup always smelled and tasted horrible, but we were all used to it," Jack said. "The soup cooked slowly all night in those huge pots. We made up a little bed in the corner and took turns sleeping, making sure one of us was always awake and alert. We took our job very seriously. The guards came and went from the kitchen, but there were times when no guards were actually in the room. When we were alone, we stole what we could for ourselves and to give to our friends."

The guards' food was cooked elsewhere and brought to the camp for Jack and Moniek to heat and serve. "When we dared, we took some of it and made a little soup for ourselves in a small pot we had found," Jack said. "There were shortages of food everywhere, and the guards' food was not much better than ours, but at least their vegetables were clean and not rotten, and their bread was not made with sawdust."

One time, they had their little pot cooking when they heard the guards coming. In a split second, the boys grabbed the pot and plopped it deep into one of the big kettles of soup. Once when loaves of the sawdust-filled bread—which was baked away from the camp—were being brought into the kitchen, Moniek distracted the guard who was counting them. Because of this, the guard ended up undercounting the delivery by ten loaves. The boys hid the extra bread under the coal beds. They kept some for themselves and slipped the rest to starving friends.

Food had become so scarce that each prisoner was issued a monthly meal ticket, which was punched when he went through the food line to prevent the possibility of someone going through the line twice. Jack and Moniek had tickets but did not need them. They gave them to friends so they could eat twice. Jack's ticket went to a tailor named Salek, who in return helped Jack by keeping his uniform clean and repaired.

Someone told camp authorities what the boys were doing—

probably a prisoner who got extra bread for informing on them. The boys were pouring water into the huge soup kettles when guards descended on the kitchen.

"We heard their boots stomping toward us outside the building," Jack said. "They stormed through the door and surrounded us, their guns pointed at us. We threw our hands in the air, certain we were going to die, though we did not know why.

"A minute later, the head commandant of the camp came in. I will never forget him. He was all shiny boots and official uniform. He was an older man, tired-looking, thin, with gray hair."

He glared at the boys. "Give me your meal tickets!" he demanded gruffly.

"We had them in our pockets," Jack said, "because we both insisted our friends give them back to us each time they used them just in case this very thing happened."

With shaking hands, they handed over the tickets. Jack knew they could still be shot. Any excuse—even an accusation that could not be proved—was enough.

But the commandant looked satisfied, perhaps even relieved. He signaled the guards, and they left without a word. Jack and Moniek collapsed in relief.

"I do not know why he spared us," Jack said. "Prisoners were killed all the time for far less. But he could tell by the low camp numbers on our uniforms that we were both old-timers. He was one himself. Maybe that was why."

Once, a horse wandered up to the camp gate. It was a skinny, bony old horse, probably diseased, but to everyone in the camp, it represented food. Prisoners who had once been butchers by trade took over. The guards got the choice meat in their soup, and Moniek and Jack added the rest to the prisoners' soup.

"That was a memorable meal," Jack recalled. "There was not much to go around, but we enjoyed it nonetheless. When you are starving, horse meat is not so bad."

12

Early one morning, when no guard was around, Moniek caught a Hungarian Jewish prisoner trying to steal potatoes. Moniek shouted at him to get out, but the man ignored him.

"We had to keep strict control in and around the kitchen, or all the prisoners would have been trying to steal food," Jack said. "Neither of us spoke Hungarian, so communicating with Hungarian prisoners was very difficult. When this man would not leave, Moniek started to push him out of the room. The man resisted, and Moniek had to hit him. He yelled and made threatening gestures. After our close call with the commandant, not much scared either of us, so we did not worry."

For two precious months, Jack and Moniek cooked the soup and served the bread from the kitchen. As Jack grew stronger and healthier, he was convinced once more that he would survive the war and be reunited with his family.

All the cold first months of 1945, rumors persisted that Russian troops were getting closer. Then one day in late March, with only a few hours' warning, prisoners were informed the camp would be evacuated and prisoners taken to another camp. Rumors immediately flew that the Russians were nearby. *No, it is the Americans coming,* said someone. *The British,* said someone else. *Hitler wants us all dead. The guards will take us to the countryside and kill us,* several prisoners declared. *Hitler is winning and needs our labor elsewhere,* insisted other prisoners.

When Jack heard news of the evacuation, he panicked. Now how would he and Moniek get the extra food that had kept them going? If they had not become the cooks, he was not sure either of them would still be alive.

The boys were ordered to load a wagon with all the kitchen supplies. "Very little food was left," Jack said. "Since we had no horse to pull the wagon, we prisoners had to do it."

A drizzly gray rain began almost as soon as the group of several hundred left the camp, headed west. The guards were covered with rain ponchos and wore coats and boots. Prisoners had only their thin uniforms and wooden shoes.

"We were soaking wet and very cold," Jack said. "The roads were mud. Those of us acting as horse for the wagon struggled to pull it through the holes on the road and up the hills and across streams. Whenever we could, we scavenged in the fields, looking for a beet or potato—anything edible. We were starving.

To prevent prisoners from being liberated by the Allies, the Nazis sent hundreds of thousands on forced death marches, regardless of weather or the health of the prisoners.

"The guards were also hungry. They prodded us to keep moving, but they lacked any enthusiasm. I do not think they knew what was happening with the war any more than we did. The only advantage they had over other soldiers was that as long as they were guarding us, they could not be sent to the front to fight."

The group straggled along, stopping when it got dark, then sleeping wherever they could find a spot by the side of the road or in a field. Several days later, they reached their destination: the Doernhau concentration camp. Like all the others, this one was surrounded with electrified barbed wire and had towers where guards with searchlights, binoculars, and machine guns kept watch on the prisoners.

Hungry and exhausted, Jack and Moniek saw that this camp was more crowded than the last. Almost all the prisoners were Hungarian Jews. Unable to communicate with them, the boys could not find out about conditions in the camp. Prisoners idled about. No one had anything to do.

As Jack and Moniek wandered through the crowded camp, a group of Hungarians suddenly surrounded them. With them was the prisoner from the last camp whom Moniek had kicked out of the kitchen. He was talking loudly to the others and gesturing at Moniek.

Two prisoners grabbed Jack and held him while the others set on Moniek, beating him savagely. Jack screamed at them to stop. One of the prisoners held his hands over Jack's mouth. *Why do the guards in the towers not see what is going on and stop this? They have always been all-seeing. Why have they stopped paying attention?* Jack wondered.

The two prisoners holding Jack dragged him into the main part of the camp, far from Moniek. With thousands of prisoners milling around, Jack quickly lost any sense of direction. Frantic, he searched until he finally found his way back to the spot where Moniek had been attacked. But neither Moniek nor the others were there. Where had his friend been taken?

Jack searched until dark, going in and out of barracks, calling

Moniek's name, but he could not find him. Inside the overcrowded barracks, starving prisoners lay crammed together on the platforms, their eyes glazed over, their emaciated bodies barely able to move. Jack realized that many of these men were ill with typhus, which explained why the guards did not come into the barracks or patrol the camp on foot but stayed at a safe distance in the guard towers. Gangs of Hungarian prisoners seemed to control the camp—and the guards did nothing.

That night, Jack and hundreds of other prisoners were ordered to sleep on a concrete floor in one of the camp buildings. They had no blankets. It was very cold. Around Jack, sick prisoners coughed and cried.

"We had been given nothing to eat," said Jack, "and after our long march, my body was already starting to weaken, even though I had gained strength while I was the cook. I was very worried about Moniek. I knew he could not be in good shape—if he was still alive."

Camp conditions were so terrible that prisoners were given one cup of soup a day, and this was really only flavored water. Several times a week, they got a little bread. Some days, there was nothing. Although roll call was held each morning, the daily death toll from typhus and starvation was quickly reducing the prisoner population. The camp crematorium belched black smoke all day and all night.

"With no work, I spent my days looking for Moniek," Jack said. "I was so weak, I worried about fainting. At night, I worried about freezing. I was covered with lice and had no way to clean myself or to wash my uniform. I could not communicate with other prisoners; I had no friends. I could do nothing for myself or for anyone else. I was sure Moniek was dead. I had never in my life felt so alone.

"I had been in this camp five or six weeks, when one day I was sitting on a stoop and the realization came over me that I had only weeks to live. I had survived in the concentration camps almost three years, and I knew that what I was feeling was what I had seen many times in men's eyes shortly before they died. I did not have the will to go on."

That night, for the first time in Jack's experience, the prisoners were locked in their barracks. They could hear Allied planes flying overhead and the occasional sound of bombs blowing up ground targets. Peeking through cracks in the walls, they could see anti-aircraft fire light up the sky. Jack knew the camp could be a target and they might be blown to bits.

He did not care. He would not live to see liberation. He cared only that the Allies were bombing Germany, and that Hitler would lose the war.

But Hitler had won the game with Jack.

The next morning, he awoke to a strange void: No kapo was yelling at him or trying to beat him over the head. Weak with fatigue and hunger, he slowly sat up. He could hear nothing outside the darkened barracks. Other prisoners were starting to stir, and Jack forced himself to stand up and look around.

Two prisoners were trying to break down the locked door. They motioned for Jack to help. Several other prisoners joined in, and with great effort, they finally broke the hinges.

Rays of daylight trickled into the room.

It could be a trap. Did they dare go outside? Were guards with machine guns waiting to shoot them all?

Jack and several others stepped outside and looked around. Seeing nothing, they signaled for the others to follow. Silently, they shuffled toward the center of the camp. Jack was the first to get a clear view of the guard towers. Empty!

He began to shout and point, and instantly the other prisoners let out a cheer and began hugging one another. They started breaking the locks off all the barracks. Soon thousands of prisoners filled the center area of the camp. They broke into the kitchen—no food. Looking through the fence, they could see the guards' and officers' housing—all empty. The doors to the administration buildings stood open.

The war was over. *It was over!* Just like that. No big battle, no surrender, no foreign troops liberating them. The guards had gone in the night, taking with them not only the dogs, their weapons, and what food was left, but even the Nazi flag that had flown from the flagpole in the center of the camp.

As Jack tried to take all this in, he felt a tap on his shoulder. As he turned, he saw red hair and a freckled face with blue eyes and faintly visible bruises. Jack folded himself into Moniek's embrace. For the first time in three years, he let himself cry.

13

THE SEARCH

imping and still stiff, and as perilously thin as Jack, Moniek quickly related how he had spent all this time lying in a far-off barracks, recovering from his injuries. "You do not want to hear about it," he said. "Nothing matters except that we are now free. We have survived, Jack! I always knew we would make it!"

The boys helped short-circuit the electric fence and open the front gates. Jack and Moniek were the first ones to walk outside. The other prisoners hung back, not believing they were free. They would wait for the Russians to liberate them.

"But Moniek and I decided to liberate ourselves," Jack said. "We could not wait a moment longer for our freedom."

It was early morning, and the road was quiet as the two boys ventured forth. Mist clung to the ground. They breathed in the soft spring air. They could hear birds singing in the trees. Jack knew they were both too weak to walk very far. Moniek limped badly. It had been at least two days since either of them had last eaten anything. Over the first hill, they saw an amazing sight: Abandoned motorcycles, trucks, and even guns littered the road, as though the Germans had dropped everything and started running. Had they heard the Russians coming? But there was no sign of troops from either side.

They walked on and found a military wagon with a horse hitched to it. They climbed aboard, laughing as they recalled their meal of horse meat, and how, on the horrible march to this last camp, *they* had been the horse.

Several miles down the road, they came to another concentration camp. No guards were in the towers. Jack and Moniek broke open the gates. Inside, sick and emaciated women—the first women Jack had seen in three years—watched fearfully from the shadows as the boys entered the camp. When the women saw their prisoner uniforms, they swarmed around them. Most of the women spoke Hungarian.

"It is over," Jack told them. "The war is over!"

Somebody quickly translated, and the women began to cheer. Many cried. Outside the gates, Jack could see a town. Food had to be the first order of business. Jack and Moniek took the wagon to the outskirts of the town. "We were filthy, our camp uniforms almost rotted off our bodies, and both of us so weak and emaciated, we could hardly stand," Jack said.

German townspeople watched them but would not talk to

Jewish survivors gather outside the infirmary barracks in Ebensee on the day after liberation.

them. People were loading up household belongings and fleeing. They saw a small German bakery and went in the open door. Jack had to resist grabbing a loaf of freshly baked bread. An old woman who had been stacking the bread stood back when she saw them, her eyes fearful.

"*Fräulein,* where are the soldiers?" Jack asked in German.

"They have run away," she replied timidly. "They say the Russians will soon be here. Hitler was very cruel to the Russian people, and everyone is afraid."

"We need bread," Moniek told her.

The woman's eyes darted to the loaves and then back at the boys. "I can see you were in that camp, yes? So you take it." She disappeared into the back room. Jack and Moniek grabbed a loaf and tore it in half, cramming it into their mouths. Jack thought he had never tasted anything so good in his life. Moniek agreed. *Real* bread, no sawdust.

"We need bread for others," Jack told the woman.

"Yes, give it to them," she said. "I am leaving anyway."

They loaded the wagon with all the bread she had. Before they left, Jack asked her the date. "May seventh, 1945," came her answer. *Liberation Day.*

Back at the women's camp, they divided up the bread. Those with enough strength devoured it quickly. Others chewed slowly. "The Russians will be here soon," the boys told them. "You can stay or not. You are free!"

But like the men at the other camp, the women did not know what to do with their freedom. The boys went back to the town and found a house whose owners had just fled, leaving everything behind.

"How can I explain what it was like to walk into a real home?" Jack said. "It was paradise. We had lice crawling on us, our bodies were mere skeletons, and we were standing in a house with potted flowers on the windowsills and embroidered doilies on polished tables. Outside, there was even a small garden, and we found a cellar with jars of canned vegetables and meats."

Jack and Moniek quickly set up housekeeping. Soon, several other liberated prisoners joined them. They found clothes in the closets to wear—*clean* clothes—which they put on after scrubbing themselves with *real* soap and drying themselves with *real* towels. Everything smelled fresh. It smelled wonderful!

"I was no longer prisoner 16013. I could not throw away that filthy uniform with that hateful number fast enough," said Jack.

They built a fire in the stove and made tea and feasted on vegetables, fried potatoes, and canned meats, eating so much, they feared they would get sick. To top it off, they found some brightly wrapped candies in a closet and savored the delicate sweet taste.

"We expected it all to end at any moment. Either the Nazis would find us and shoot us or it was a dream and we would wake up," Jack said. "Instead, Russian troops arrived later that day, and they quickly occupied the entire area. They wished us good luck and told us to stay as long as we liked."

That night, a clean, well-fed Jack slept for the first time in three years in a bed with sheets, a feather pillow cradling his head. In the middle of the night, he left the bed to sleep on the floor because the bed was too soft. He awoke the next morning when he felt like it.

For several days, they stayed in the house. The Russian troops could see from their appearance what they had been through and were kind to them, but they had only a little bread to give them.

"Food was the major problem," Jack said. "Nobody had any. Moniek and I and some other prisoners quickly used up all the food we had found."

Allied bombing raids destroyed strategic locations throughout Europe in the push to defeat Hitler.

Much of Germany was in ruins. Hitler had committed suicide, and his generals had either killed themselves, been arrested, or gone into hiding. The victorious Allies divided Germany into four occupied zones: Russian, French, British, and American.

"Moniek and I had two main objectives," said Jack. "To regain our health—which meant we had to go where there was food—and to find our families."

When they heard the Americans had the most food, they walked and hitched rides on Allied military trucks to the bombed-out city of Frankfurt, which was in the American zone. In a village near the city, they found a displaced persons' camp set up at a former military base to provide temporary shelter and help for war victims and refugees. They settled in, sharing a room. When they were checked over by a doctor, Jack, who was now eighteen, stood five seven and weighed 80 pounds. The last time he had known his weight, he was twelve years old, was several inches shorter, and weighed 110 pounds. His teeth had suffered so much from malnutrition and lack of care that seven eventually had to be pulled.

The boys registered with groups organizing to help people find one another. Daily lists were posted of people looking for someone. Every day, the boys scanned the ever-growing lists for familiar names. As they talked to people, they began to understand the hardships suffered by so many during the almost six years that the war had ravaged Europe. But little matched the horrors of the concentration camps and gas chambers.

"Moniek and I were actually lucky our last camp had had a typhus epidemic, because it kept the guards out," Jack said. "In many camps, guards slaughtered the prisoners before they ran away. Former prisoners told of being on harrowing death marches where almost everyone died along the way from exhaustion and exposure, and stragglers were shot. We did not experience that, either."

Moniek was eventually reunited with both of his brothers. One had been in the camps, and the other with Polish troops that had escaped to Russia to help fight the Germans. The three brothers learned their two sisters and their parents were dead. They decided to try their luck away from Frankfurt, and Jack and Moniek bid each other a tearful good-bye.

"I owed Moniek my survival. He had helped me in so many ways, and his optimism kept me going through the darkest days," Jack said. "I knew he needed to be with his brothers, and that we would always be in touch. But parting was painful after what we had been through together."

When Moniek left, Jack moved out of the camp and into a private home. A German woman whose husband had not returned from the war lived there with her young child and her elderly mother. In exchange for his room and laundry services, Jack gave the women extra food rations he got from the Americans.

"The world had little sympathy for the suffering of the German people after the war," said Jack. "This woman had no way to support her mother and child, and I felt sorry for her. She was very grateful for the little I could do for her. I do not know if her husband ever came back."

Each day, he reported to the displaced persons' camp to get food rations, army-surplus clothes, or other supplies, and to search the lists. One day, he saw the name Arek Mandelbaum. He found the man, and together they figured out that their grandfathers were brothers, making the two of them second cousins. Arek's brother Robert had also survived. Arek said that Jack's uncle Sigmund, his father's younger brother, was alive and staying in a displaced persons' camp near Munich.

Travel was almost at a standstill for the first few months after the war. Few trains were running, and many roads were still in ruins. With great difficulty, Jack made his way to Munich and found his uncle. Their reunion was emotional.

"He had been in Auschwitz and had suffered a great deal, but I recognized him, for he still had his bald head and rosy cheeks," Jack said.

He also had devastating news.

"Your father is dead, Jack," he said gently. "I was transferred to the Stutthof concentration camp just a month before liberation, and I met friends of his, who told me that he had died the day before I arrived."

"I insisted it could not be true, that my father was invincible," Jack said, "though in my heart, I knew my uncle would not lie to me. It took me a long time to accept that my beloved papa was truly gone."

Jack continued his search for other family members. One day while walking on a street in the displaced persons' camp, he thought he recognized a woman's voice. She went into a building before Jack could see her face, so he waited until she came out. When she did, they fell into each other's arms. It was Aunt Hinda, his mother's spoiled youngest sister, who used to stay with the family. Jack learned his aunt had been married two years before she was deported to Auschwitz and had since been reunited with her husband.

"It was hard for me to believe that someone who was once as pampered as she had been, who had never worked, could survive

Wearing a jacket his aunt's husband, a tailor, made for him from a U.S. Army surplus blanket, Jack had this photo taken of himself shortly after his liberation.

Auschwitz, while my father had died," Jack said. "But that was the luck of who made it and who did not. Her husband was a tailor, and he made me a coat from a U.S. Army blanket, which I wore in the first photo I had taken after the war."

As soon as he could arrange it, Jack made his first trip back to Poland to search for the rest of his family. In the year following the war, he would make this journey three times, returning after each trip to the American sector of Germany, where he could count on food, and where the Red Cross and United Nations continued to work at reuniting family members.

"Travel into Poland was almost impossible," Jack recalled. "The few trains running were very crowded. All the windows were smashed out, and people hung off the sides and even climbed up on the roof. Bridges were bombed out, so the train would stop on one side of the river and you would have to make your way across a bridge half sunk in water and then board another train on the other side. Everything was in chaos and ruins."

Jack's hometown of Gdynia looked the same, for although Hitler had used its ports, the Allies had not bombed it. But Jack found hostile strangers in the family's old apartment. All their belongings had been looted by townspeople and the Nazis, and now the government had taken over his father's fish cannery.

In Grandfather's town, the house with the upstairs balcony, where he had watched the Nazis arrive six years earlier, was also occupied by strangers. Townspeople told Jack how the Nazis had deported most of the Jewish population, loading them into boxcars, never to be heard from again.

And Grandfather? The story came out haltingly, the townspeople shamed by what had happened. About two thousand elderly Jews, including Grandfather and his wife, had been marched to a ravine outside town and shot. Their bodies were dumped into an enormous common grave.

"But the one allotted bullet per person was not always enough to kill instantly," Jack said. "I was told the earth over the grave moved for two days."

In the village where Jack's sister, Jadzia, had lived with their aunt and uncle while caring for their baby, Jack was able to learn his sister's fate from neighbors. Early in 1942, the Nazis had rounded up all the Jewish adults in the village and deported them to the death camps. The aunt and uncle had been taken, and Jadzia was left to care for the baby. Late in 1942, the Nazis had conducted a second roundup.

"According to these neighbors, my sister was told that if she would leave the child, she could go to a labor camp. Had she done so, perhaps she would have survived. But she would not abandon the baby; she went, instead, to the gas chambers, the baby in her arms. She was seventeen years old."

The trip to his uncle's village revealed the final chapter of his family's fate.

"I learned from the villagers that once those of us selected to go to the concentration camp had left on the trucks, everyone else, including my uncle and his family and my mother and my brother, Jakob, was locked inside the brewery. They were kept there for three days without food or water. The third day, they were marched about four miles to the local train station and put into cattle cars for the journey to Auschwitz.

"It was only half a day's ride. Probably Mama and Jakob were taken to the gas chambers that very day. In my heart, I know Mama was holding my little brother's hand as they died."

Jack could not accept the finality of his family's murder. Wherever he traveled, he found himself looking into faces, thinking maybe there had been a mistake, that one of them had survived. He would do this for the next fifty years.

"You never get over something like this," Jack said. "It haunts you every day of your life. I still wonder, *Could Papa have survived one more month if he had known liberation was that close? What if Jadzia had left the baby? What went through Mama's mind as they slammed the door of the gas chamber?*

"There was nothing left for me in Europe. There were too many bad memories. I wanted to leave. I could not get out of there fast enough."

Before the war, Jack had had parents, a brother, a sister, a grandfather, uncles, aunts, and cousins—eighty people in all. Now, everyone except Jack's second cousins, Robert and Arek, Aunt Hinda, Uncle Sigmund, and Jack was dead. Hitler and his millions of willing accomplices had succeeded in destroying a family once vibrant, prosperous, and loving.

"If I had known this when I was in the camps," Jack said sadly, "why would I have struggled so hard to live?"

14

CREATING A NEW LIFE

A year after his liberation, Jack had his paperwork in hand to go to the United States. The American president, Harry Truman, had petitioned Congress to allow tens of thousands of concentration camp survivors to immigrate to the United States. In June 1946, Jack and six hundred other survivors boarded a U.S. military troop ship to cross the Atlantic. In his group were his uncle, his second cousins Arek and Robert Mandelbaum, and six other survivors. All together, the group spoke only a few words of English. The Jewish resettlement official with the Joint Distribution Committee who met them when they landed in New York City on June 24, 1946, suggested Kansas City as a destination. They were each given five dollars and a train ticket.

Within days of arriving in Kansas City, Jack had a job working for a clothing-distribution wholesaler, sweeping floors and moving boxes. Uncle Sigmund worked as a painter. They shared a rented

Jack and Claudia posed in the mid-1990s with their seven children, the spouses of several, and their first two grandchildren.

room and took English classes at night at the Jewish Community Center. In 1952, Jack became an American citizen. He worked hard and saved every cent he could until he was able to bring Aunt Hinda, her husband, and the daughter since born to them to Kansas City.

Ten years after arriving in America, Jack took out a loan, bought the company he was working for, and turned it into a thriving import company. Later, he started a successful investment business. He also married. Today, he and his wife, Claudia, have seven children and twelve grandchildren.

On business trips, Jack was sometimes able to see Moniek, who moved to the United States in 1950, settled in New York State, and worked in the construction business. Moniek married, and he and his wife, Erica, reared two sons before retiring to Florida. He has never returned to Europe. "I would not go for a million dollars," he said. "I did not do anything wrong, and look what happened to me. I was a kid, I went to school, and then the Nazis came in and destroyed my family. I will never set foot in that place again."

He and Jack have always stayed in touch. "When we were in the camps, I would have done anything for him, and he would have done anything for me," Moniek said. "Jack was a true friend."

Once when Jack attended an event for Holocaust survivors, he was told someone was looking for him. It was Salek, the tailor Jack had given his meal card to when he and Moniek were the cooks. Salek embraced him warmly. "Without that extra food, I would not have survived. You saved my life, Jack," Salek told him.

Jack lost his aunt Hinda to cancer fifteen years after she came to Kansas City. "She did not want to talk about the Holocaust," Jack said, "so I did not push her. But I wish I had gotten more family history from her before she died. So much is lost."

Uncle Sigmund married, fathered two daughters, and eventually owned a small grocery store until his retirement. In 1999, when he was eighty-nine years old, Jack took him to visit Poland for the first time since the war and was with him as he laid a wreath before the monument commemorating the massacre in which his father,

Moniek after the war

who was Jack's grandfather, was murdered. During their visit to Auschwitz, which is now a museum, Uncle Sigmund shared his memories of being assigned to repaint the gas chambers after each mass execution.

"I think it was very good for him to go there and to talk about it finally," Jack said.

For Jack, that trip was the eighth time he had visited Poland since

Uncle Sigmund after the war

the war in his effort to come to terms with what had happened to him and to reconstruct what family history he could. Almost all records were destroyed in the war. Family photos also disappeared. Today, Jack has only a photo of his father once sent to a cousin in Israel (see page 11), and a photo of his mother's sister Tauba, which had also been sent to a cousin (see page 8).

"She looked very much like my mother, so at least I have that," he said. "When my children were growing up, they knew only that I came from Europe and had lost my family. They knew no details

The summer of 1999 Jack took his uncle Sigmund, then eighty-nine, to visit Poland for the first time since the war. At Auschwitz, where Uncle Sig was a prisoner, they stood before the entrance to the gas chamber. Uncle Sig had to repaint the chamber after each mass execution. Uncle Sig's tattoo, put on him at Auschwitz, is visible on his left arm.

for thirty years because I did not want to burden them.

"Besides, you cannot talk about history until you can step back for a long time to look at it. I was building a business and raising a family, and I pushed back the memories."

Jack called the decades he devoted to his family and business "time for the stomach." Then came "time for the soul." For many years, Jack assisted Jewish immigrants coming into Kansas City, helping them to get settled. He has always been deeply involved in issues related to Holocaust survivors. In 1993, he and his close friend Isak Federman, a Polish Jew and a camp survivor who was on the same boat to America as Jack, realized a long-cherished dream. With encouragement and support from their families, they cofounded the Midwest Center for Holocaust Education. They wanted to help people learn about the Holocaust, and to work for understanding and compassion among all races and religions. The center includes a reference library of Holocaust materials and a speakers' bureau.

"One thing people wonder is why the Jews did not defend themselves, why we were like lambs led to the slaughter. In truth, many Jews fought back bravely. But the Holocaust was so well planned that we were overwhelmed," Jack said. "It started with little acts of racism and discrimination and eventually led to the murders of millions of innocents. We thought the European people would rise up out of basic decency and defend us. Some tried, but not enough. We must never think the Holocaust cannot happen again."

Jack frequently speaks to schoolchildren and to civic groups. He tells them about his boyhood in Gdynia and leads them gradually into his experiences in the camps. They sit quietly, absorbing his story, and then flood him with questions.

"Many survivors will not speak out because it is too painful for them to remember. It is painful for me, as well," Jack said. "It exhausts me, and afterward I have difficulty sleeping. Sometimes, I dream I am back in the camps and I am freezing and starving. Sometimes, I dream I die, drowned in a ditch or shot by a guard.

"Then I wake up—a wonderful feeling—and I understand that I must speak for all those who cannot speak for themselves. Something good must come from their sacrifice. So I speak, hoping I can make a difference. This is my memorial to my family."

Most survivors suffer physical problems associated with long periods of deprivation. Jack's have been mild compared with those of many others—circulation problems in his feet because of repeated frostbite, and arthritis and rheumatism in his back.

"It is amazing how much misery the human body can tolerate," Jack said. "On a recent winter morning, I put on a heavy coat, hat, gloves, and boots to go outside to the driveway for the newspaper. And I wondered, How did I survive those winters when I had only a thin uniform to wear while I worked outdoors all day doing heavy labor?"

Greater than the physical suffering is the emotional. "Almost all of us suffer from post-traumatic stress syndrome," Jack said. "At the Jewish Community Center day school, I sometimes see preschoolers lined up with their teacher. I tremble, remembering that the Germans marched little ones just like that to the gas chambers."

People assume, as the survivors grow older, they put their suffering behind them. It is the exact opposite, Jack said. "The enormity of the crime becomes more intolerable because you have time to think about it.

"I know of a survivor who went through the same kind of selection I did that day I was separated from my mother and brother, only he and his younger brother were put to one side, while their parents were on the other. He thought the adults were the ones being taken to work, while the younger ones would be killed. He told his brother to try to sneak back to their parents. The boy did—and he and his parents went to the gas chambers. This man has never forgiven himself. There are a million stories like that.

"In spite of all the terrible things that happened to me, I did not allow Hitler to make me feel less than human. I had been raised well and I knew who I was. My strategy was *not* to allow myself to hate. I knew I could be consumed by such hate.

"I have known many survivors for whom the Holocaust is the central theme of their lives. They have no other. I have tried to live with tolerance and forgiveness as the themes of my life.

"God gave us the power to be good or evil. This is our choice. Because some pick evil, we must work together to recognize and stop it. But while we survivors may lead the charge, we cannot do this alone. It must be the goal of all people.

"If we will join in this goal, then there is hope for humanity."

To the memory
of the men, women, and children
who fell victim to the Nazi genocide.
Here lie their ashes.
May their souls rest in peace.

A testament to the dead at Auschwitz

"There are many lessons one can learn from my father's story. But for me, one of the most important lessons has always been that extraordinary people are simply ordinary people, like my father, who rose to the challenge in an extraordinary crisis."

—John Mandelbaum
Jack's son

THE CONCENTRATION CAMPS

The Nazis set up a complex system of camps throughout Europe. Some were prisoner-of-war camps; others were slave-labor or killing camps. Some had only a few hundred prisoners, and others had as many as fifty thousand. There may have been as many as nine thousand concentration camps, many of them smaller satellite camps of larger ones. With the exception of Blechhammer, the first concentration camp Jack was in, all the others he was in were satellite camps of the Gross-Rosen concentration camp. All of these were fairly close to one another and were in the vicinity of the city of Breslau, then in eastern Germany, now in western Poland and named Wroclaw.

The camps established to intern prisoners were usually built with the cheapest materials possible. Barracks were built of wood or concrete slabs, with wooden or concrete floors. Some camps were converted factories or stables.

Inside the electrified barbed-wire fences and guard stations that surrounded every camp were the barracks, a kitchen, latrines, and a large, bare, open yard where prisoners lined up for roll call. Outside the fence, but usually on the camp grounds, were the guards' and officers' quarters, storage facilities, and the administration area.

Some camps were located in very isolated areas, and some were on the ouskirts of communities.

The elite SS troops of Hitler's army ran the concentration camps as a profitable business. In addition to the labor that prisoners contributed to the Nazi war effort, the SS leased prisoners to factories and businesses, collecting payment for each of them. How much was paid sometimes depended on the perceived value of the prisoner's labor. (According to surviving records, Jack's labor was often worth twice as much as that of other prisoners.)

In order to keep track of prisoners, the Nazis had an elaborate bookkeeping system in many camps, where they recorded entry dates, health information, work information, and dates of transfers or death. New prisoners were assigned numbers, which were affixed to their uniforms. In some camps, prisoners were tattooed with their numbers, beginning with low numbers and progressing to higher ones. Camp record-keeping systems noted prisoners' numbers and sometimes their names, as well.

For Jewish prisoners, all the concentration camps were death camps. The only way a person left them was by dying—from overwork, starvation, disease, brutal punishment, or execution. There were also camps where newly arrived transports of people went through a "selection" process, where they were sent to a group on the right or the left, to life or to death. Those given the death sign were taken directly to the gas chambers. At Auschwitz alone, which was part slave-labor camp and part killing camp, over

1.25 million people were murdered at the hands of the Nazis. Ninety percent were Jewish.

At the killing camps, victims were usually gassed within twenty-four hours of their arrival. Some of the more notorious killing camps were Belzec, Sobibor, Treblinka, Chelmno, Majdanek, and Auschwitz-Birkenau.

When the Nazis realized they would lose the war, they did not want survivors telling what had happened. Many prisoners were killed. Others were taken on forced marches, which were actually death marches since few of the freezing, starving prisoners survived them.

Today, some of the camps have become museums, where visitors can see the barracks, the gas chambers, and the crematoriums—sober reminders of one of the blackest marks on human history.

Girls in the Camps

Along with young children, the Nazis usually killed their mothers and older sisters. Girls and women who were strong and healthy and were not trying to care for a child had the possibility of being placed in labor camps. There they worked in factories or on farms, and did heavy outdoor work. They were supervised by female guards and kapos, who could be every bit as brutal as their male counterparts.

In some camps, females wore sacklike dresses. In others, they wore the same striped uniforms as males. Like males, they had their heads and bodies shaved and deloused. Camp conditions for females were very similar to what boys and men endured, but far fewer girls and women were able to survive them.

Children in the Holocaust

The Nazis viewed children as a liability and showed them no mercy. It is estimated that less than 10 percent of Europe's Jewish children under the age of sixteen survived the Holocaust. The Nazis also targeted Gypsy children and all children with mental or physical disabilities. Many other children starved to death during the war.

When the Nazis rounded up families, if they wanted to use the parents as laborers, children were sent to the gas chambers alone, or were shot and buried in mass graves.

In some instances, children were allowed to go to the camps with their parents. Some children were even sent to camps by themselves. Older children, provided they were healthy and strong, were put to work. Because conditions in the camps were so bad, most children eventually succumbed to starvation or disease.

Nobody knows how many Jewish children went into hiding. Figures range from 10,000 to 100,000. Many of these children were hidden in monasteries and convents, on remote farms, in secret rooms in houses, or in underground sewers. They were never totally safe.

Before the war started, some children were sent to other countries for safety reasons. Under a program called *Kindertransport,* several thousand German and Austrian Jewish children were sent to Great

Britain, the United States, and Palestine (now Israel) before the war started. Most never saw their parents again.

The war left many children orphans. Some of these children had seen their families murdered. Many did not know the fate of their families and spent years looking for them. Some children were not orphaned, but because of the war, they lost contact with their families. Regardless of the circumstances, most of these children suffered long-term effects of stress, loss, fear, and trauma. Some went to live with relatives after the war. Others stayed in children's centers established in Europe after the war and grew up there. Once they were teenagers, many moved to Palestine, Great Britain, Australia, Canada, or the United States.

The Human Cost of World War II
An estimated 55 million people died in World War II.
- Only 17 million were soldiers; the rest were civilians.
- Approximately 500,000 Gypsies*—one third of their population—were murdered by the Nazis.
- Eleven million people were murdered in the Nazi death camps.
- Over 6 million of Europe's 8.6 million Jews were murdered between 1933 and 1945.
- Of Poland's prewar Jewish population of 3.5 million, only 10 percent survived.

*The correct name for these people is Roma or Sinti. Hitler persecuted them because they were a dark-skinned ethnic minority he considered inferior.

MULTIMEDIA RECOMMENDATIONS

Sources Used in This Book

Education materials from the United States Holocaust Memorial Museum, Washington, DC; *Encyclopedia of the Holocaust*, volumes 1–4, editor in chief, Israel Gutman, (New York: Macmillan, 1990); Jack R. Fischel, *The Holocaust* (Westport, CT: Greenwood Press, 1998); Seymour Rossel, *The Holocaust: The World and the Jews, 1933–1945* (West Orange, NJ: Behrman House, Inc., 1992).

Books for Grades 6–9

Anne Frank: The Diary of a Young Girl (New York: Pocket Books, 1953). Anne was thirteen when her family went into hiding in Amsterdam and she started her diary, which was found after Anne had already been shipped to a concentration camp, where she died.

The Hidden Children by Howard Greenfeld (New York: Ticknor & Fields, 1993). Thirteen Holocaust survivors tell their true childhood stories of surviving the Nazis by staying out of their reach.

I Never Saw Another Butterfly: Children's Drawings and Poems from Terezin Concentration Camp, 1942–1944 (New York: Schocken, 1993). A moving collection of poetry and drawings by children in the Terezin concentration camp outside Prague.

Jacob's Rescue: A Holocaust Story by Malka Drucker and Michael Halperin (New York: Bantam, 1993). Fiction based on a true story of a Jewish boy in Warsaw who was hidden during the war by a non-Jewish family.

No Pretty Pictures: A Child of War by Anita Lobel (New York: Greenwillow, 1998). A nonfiction account of the artist's Jewish childhood in Poland as she tried to elude the Nazis.

Number the Stars by Lois Lowry (Boston: Houghton Mifflin, 1989). The fictional story of how a Danish girl helped protect her Danish Jewish friend when the Nazis invaded Denmark.

Tell Them We Remember: The Story of the Holocaust by Susan D. Bachrach (Boston: Little, Brown, 1994). A photo history produced under the auspices of the United States Holocaust Memorial Museum, this book explains in clear language the Holocaust's impact on children and young people.

Books for Older Readers

All but My Life by Gerda Weissmann Klein (New York: Hill and Wang, 1957). True story of a Polish Jewish girl in the Holocaust.

—And God Cried: The Holocaust Remembered by Charles Lawliss (New York: JG Press, 1994). A clearly written history of the Jews and the Holocaust.

Bearing Witness: Stories of the Holocaust selected by Hazel Rochman and Darlene Z. McCampbell (New York: Orchard Books, 1995). This slender volume comprises some of the best writings about the Holocaust from such acclaimed writers as Elie Wiesel, Primo Levi, Cynthia Ozick, and Frank O'Connor.

I Have Lived a Thousand Years: Growing Up in the Holocaust by Livia Bitton-Jackson (New York: Simon & Schuster, 1997). True story of a thirteen-year-old during 1944–1945, when the Nazis invaded Hungary.

Night by Elie Wiesel (New York: Bantam, 1982). A devastating journey with Nobel Prize recipient Wiesel and his father into the concentration camps.

A Nightmare in History: The Holocaust 1933–1945 by Miriam Chaikin (Boston: Houghton Mifflin/Clarion, 1987). An excellent overview of the Holocaust and why it happened.

We Are Witnesses: Five Diaries of Teenagers Who Died in the Holocaust by Jacob Boas (New York: Scholastic, 1996). The actual diaries of five diverse Jewish teenagers from different parts of Europe who perished during the Holocaust.

Films and Documentaries (Recommended for Older Students)

The Devil's Arithmetic. Based on the novel by Jane Yolen. The story of a sixteen-year-old who is transported in time from present-day life in the United States to a concentration camp during the war.

The Diary of Anne Frank. Based on the Pulitzer Prize–winning play, starring Millie Perkins as Anne.

The Last Days. A documentary that views the Holocaust through the eyes of five Hungarian concentration camp survivors. Includes rare archival footage.

One Survivor Remembers. Oscar-winning documentary about Gerda Weissman Klein, a Polish Jewish girl in the Holocaust.

Schindler's List. Steven Spielberg's Oscar-winning true story of a German businessman who saved the lives of many concentration camp prisoners.

Software

Survivors: Testimonies of the Holocaust. An interactive CD-ROM in which four survivors tell their stories. Produced by the Shoah Foundation. Winona Ryder and Leonardo DiCaprio narrate.

Websites

Many websites are devoted to the Holocaust and to specialized topics related to the Holocaust. Three sites are highly recommended and can lead users to many other sites:

United States Holocaust Memorial Museum, Washington, DC
> www.ushmn.org/
>> To send e-mail questions or inquiries to their Education Department: education@ushmm.org
>> The museum can be contacted at
>>> 100 Raoul Wallenberg Place SW
>>> Washington, DC 20024–2126
>>> Tel.: 202 488–0400

Simon Wiesenthal Center's Museum of Tolerance, Los Angeles, CA
> www.wiesenthal.com

Holocaust Martyrs' and Heroes' Remembrance Authority, Jerusalem, Israel
> www.yad-vashem.org.il/

Another useful site is that of the Midwest Center for Holocaust Education:

www.mchekc.org
5801 West 115th Street, Suite 106
Overland Park, KS 66211–1800
Tel.: 913 327–8190
Fax: 913 327–8193

PHOTO SOURCES

Illustrations appear courtesy of the following: page 25, AP/Wide World Photos; page 22, Beth Hatefuthsoth Photo Archive, Tel Aviv, Israel; pages 32 and 36, Bundesarchiv; pages iv, 8, 11, 14, 23, 29, 74, 75, 79, 115, 120, 122, 123, 124, and 129, Jack and Claudia Mandelbaum; page 21, by Jerry Ficowski, United States Holocaust Memorial Museum (USHMM) Photo Archives; pages 6, 13, and 18, by George Fogelson, USHMM Photo Archives; pages 17 and 39, by Richard Freimark, USHMM Photo Archives; pages 26, 35, 43, and 66, Instytyt Pamieci Narodowej/Institute of National Memory, USHMM Photo Archives; page xiv, by Rose Zaks Kaplovitz, USHMM Photo Archives; page 101, KZ Gedenkstatte Dachau, USHMM Photo Archives; page 111, KZ Gedenkstatte Neuengamme, USHMM Photo Archives; page 73, Frank Manucci, USHMM Photo Archives; pages 28, 44, 77, and 108, National Archives, USHMM Photo Archives; page 83, Leopold Page Photographic Collection, USHMM Photo Archives; page 58, by Robert A. Schmuhl, USHMM Photo Archives; pages 47, 48, 49, 69, and 90, Yad Vashem Photo Archives, USHMM Photo Archives.

INDEX

religious prisoners, in concentration
    camps, 64
roll call, in concentration camps, 57, **58**,
    78, 89
rumors, and information, 73, 93–94, 100
Russian prisoners, 78, 79
Russian troops, 100, 106, 107, 108, 110

S

Salek, a tailor (friend), 96, 121
Sander, Sam, 1, 2
selection process, in camps, 46–47, **47**,
    48, **49**, 127, 134
slave labor, 38
slave-labor camps, 133
Soviet Union, 40
SS (special forces), 51, 57–58, 65, 134
starvation, 91, 93, 94, 103
Stutthof concentration camp, 27, 114
survival, effects of, 2–3, 125–27, 137
survival strategies, 59, 63, 64, 67, 68, 72,
    80

T

Truman, Harry, 119
typhus, 62, 70, 93, 103

U

uniforms, of prisoners, 52, **69**, 135
United States
  immigration to, 17, 119
  and *Kindertransport*, 136–37

W

women, in concentration camps, **69**, **83**,
    107, 109, 135–36
work details, in camps, 58–59, 75–78, **77**,
    86, 91, 93, 94–98
work projects, and civilians, 35–40, 76
World War I, 15
World War II, 19, 25, 137

Y

Yiddish language, 15, 69